Abingdon Pottery Artware

1934-1950

Stepchild of
the
Great
Depression

Joe
Paradis

Schiffer Publishing Ltd

77 Lower Valley Road, Atglen, PA 19310

To my brothers, Tom and Bob: for the love never said, the time never spent.

Printed in China

ISBN: 0-7643-0056-3

Book Design by Audrey L. Whiteside

Published by Schiffer Publishing, Ltd.
77 Lower Valley Road
Atglen, PA 19310
Phone: (610) 593-1777
Fax: (610) 593-2002
Please write for a free catalog.
This book may be purchased from the publisher.
Please include $2.95 for shipping.
Try your bookstore first.

We are interested in hearing from authors
with book ideas on related subjects.

TABLE OF CONTENTS

ACKNOWLEDGMENTS

"No man is an island, entire of itself..." wrote the poet John Donne. And no author writes a book alone. After I began writing this book, dealers and collectors from all over the country as well as interested people from my home town of Avon, Illinois, and the communities surrounding Abingdon contacted me to provide support and encouragement, some of whom I had not heard from in over thirty years. Their efforts, more than mine, made this book what it is. The only hesitation I have in naming people is the thought that I may forget someone.

A special thanks to three distinguished people: Vice Admiral James B. Stockdale USN (ret), Mrs. Frances J. Moody, and Harvey Duke. Admiral Stockdale not only read my manuscript but also took the time to develop a detailed letter and supporting documentation as well as to make numerous follow-up calls to ensure that I had what I needed from him.

Mrs. Moody was a member of the unusually talented pool of artists and designers that developed ideas for the Abingdon Pottery Artware Division from 1934 to 1941. She provided many hours of her time in interviews and telephone conversations in addition to reading and responding to correspondence.

Harvey Duke, author of several books on American pottery and a columnist for trade periodicals, has been a special help. He provided expertise and counsel on the progress of my manuscript and spent many hours reviewing and discussing my work. He also provided valuable coaching on the ins and outs of writing a book and the accepted conventions of the publishing industry. His input improved the manuscript considerably.

Thanks to M. L. "Bud" Crumbaker for his letter and insight. Thanks to all those like him who worked day after day at the Pottery during the artware era to make the artware and to manage the affairs of that small company. This must include Howard Ulhman who worked there in the late 1930s, George and Toot Boyd both who worked there more than four decades each, and Lloyd Petrie who was partially responsible for many of the glazes developed for the artware. Pete, George, Howard, and Toot (would you like to be called Vincel?)

spent time on the phone talking to me about glazes and about Abingdon Lore.

Those in and around the Abingdon community who helped me were legion. Marie Olinger was the first to encourage me to write a book. She provided information and support during those early days before even I knew that I would do this. Mrs. Edith Lewis, the wife of John Lewis and the daughter of Raymond Bidwell, provided me with copies of Mr. Lewis's writings and permission to use her original copies of the artware catalogs published by the Abingdon Potteries. Audrey Sherman provided untold time, encouragement, and information, talking to me on the phone, writing me letters, sending me valuable photographs, giving me names of others to contact, encouraging others to talk to me, reviewing my manuscripts, and generally being the fine example of charity and goodwill that is equally portrayed by people whom I mentioned before Audrey and shall mention after.

One such person is Betty Alexander who was a co-worker of Audrey's for many years and who provided me with documents, photographs, and encouragement, all of which was of value and all of which I appreciated receiving.

Bob and Edith Andrews, two veteran collectors, provided information about the history of the Pottery. Mr. Andrews's dad worked there many years and Bob related some of the production methods used by his dad in the years before the Artware Division was created (most people from the communities surrounding Abingdon who contributed to this book had a relative who worked at the Pottery or worked there themselves at one time).

Robert Rush, official Abingdon Pottery Collector's Club historian, was also generous with his time and expertise. His wit, hospitality, and generosity were enjoyed by myself and my wife, Joyce, during our photo session. His many responses to my letters and phone conversations are also appreciated.

Elaine Westover, an Abingdon Pottery Collector's Club official, provided newspaper articles that she and others had written about Abingdon. She also allowed me to photograph her collection and spent considerable time on the phone answering my questions and giving me names of others to interview and made suggestions on my manuscript. Diane Beetler, another accomplished journalist and Pottery Club official, also provided me research material, spent considerable time on the phone, and did a thorough job of reviewing my manuscript and making valuable suggestions.

Betty Way, a staff member of the Abingdon Argus, provided information about Abingdon history and Abingdon Pottery personnel that proved useful. Mike and Nancy Legate shared their enthusiasm and knowledge and provided encouragement. Brian and Anita Hickok were the first to introduce me to a large collection and to provide me with initial direction in my research. Anita's mother, Mrs. Doris Schisler, was one of the first people I interviewed. She was most gracious with her time and provided me with many names of people who proved helpful (Audrey Sherman, for example). Doris also provided background material that helped me understand more about "Abingdon Lore" or the rich tradition of stories that are kept alive and cherished by those who have lived in and around Abingdon all their lives.

Many former residents who are currently living all across the country—the Abingdon Diaspora, if you will—provided input, names and encouragement. As many of them as I can remember are: Bill Castle, Marjorie Castle, Susan Butler, Kay Hartley, Walter and Martha Honigman, Cleve Gillenwater, Mrs. C. L. Ross. Former residents from Avon and Roseville who provided encouragement and information are Dr. and Mrs. Sharon L. Bower. Phyllis Fritz, proprietor of General Store Antiques in Galesburg, Illinois, also provided encouragement —Phyllis specializes in Abingdon and has reasonable prices.

Betty Perry of Galesburg, Illinois, provided me with information about rare pieces that I was unable to find elsewhere. The same for Kathy Cleer from Ipava, Illinois, who provided information about the Abingdon Mammy cookie jar. Mrs. Harriet Goff, of Knoxville, Illinois, provided access to and information about the collection of artware at the Knoxville Museum.

Ruby Mitchell of Avon, Illinois, sent me letters of encouragement and spent time looking over several drafts of my manuscript and making valuable suggestions. Ruby provided me with the name of Wayne Allen, a knowledgeable collector from Galesburg, Illinois. Wayne reviewed my manuscript and provided encouragement and support as well as insight on the relative rarity of many pieces.

Audrey Staggs and Shirley Clayton, both who worked with my mom at Saunder's Hospital in the 1960s, called and sent me letters of encouragement and names of

people who might have pottery to photograph. Thanks for the interest and the kind words about my mother.

A special thanks to Jamie and Christine Boone for their support, their friendship, and the expertise they brought to bear that helped verify the data in this book. The Boones, like the Hickoks and the Legates, are of the younger generation of collectors with deep roots in the Abingdon area—all three couples have developed extensive expertise on the technical aspects of collecting as well as the Abingdon Lore that is as rewarding to seek out and collect as the artware itself. Christine and Jamie took considerable time to review the technical details of my manuscript. Christine's impressive editorial skills and Jamie's All-American affability made a wonderful combination as Christine's comments were as valuable and as direct as any provided.

Of the many dealers who provided input, several specialized in Abingdon Pottery and provided help in pricing and in viewing rare pieces. Frank Weldi and Mary Weldi-Skinner, proprietors of Weldi-Skinner Antiques in Chicago, Illinois, provided input on collecting and pricing and provided access to rare pieces. Mercedes DiRenzo, proprietor of Jazze Junk Antiques in Chicago, Illinois, provided assistance in developing the prices for cookie jars. Nick Bizzoni and Jack Lundgren of Poplar Grove, Illinois, also helped in developing a price guide in addition to reviewing and commenting on my manuscript. Their specialized expertise and their good humor are very much appreciated.

Barbara Nyboer, manager of the Farm Village Antique Mall in Okemos, Michigan, and proprietor of Somewhere In Time Antiques of Holt, Michigan, is an antique dealer who also specializes in Abingdon. Ms. Nyboer's expertise proved beneficial as she provided input on the text that helped considerably. Jack Murnane, another dealer from Chicago, Illinois, provided access to a most unusual piece of pottery so that it could be photographed for this collection. Ed Blas, a collector and friend from Buffalo, New York, provided input, as did Bunny Walker, a dealer from Bucyrus, Ohio, and Velmajane Cox, another dealer from Duncansville, Pennsylvania. Kathleen Moloney, author and collector from New York City, supplied pricing information and pictures of cookie jars.

Kathleen Mercer Reed, a collector, provided research material, as she had been contemplating writing a book on Abingdon and had gathered information. George Anderson and David Nottingham, both of Opequon Art Pottery Antiques in Martinsburg, West Virginia, provided editorial suggestions as well as encouragement and names of other dealers who they thought might provide input. Their friendship, input, and support are appreciated. Patti Bourgeois of Patti's Past Perfect Pottery in Westport, Massachusetts, provided encouragement and a New England/East Coast perspective on pricing while Lynda Heins and John Pecha, proprietors of Heins Pottery Plus in St. Augustine, Florida, provided a perspective from that part of the country.

In the academic community, Rena London, an author and educator from the Dallas, Texas, area provided research in the form of a manuscript that she began in the early 1980s. She also provided encouragement, support, and displayed an infectious excitement about a book on Abingdon Pottery. She had talked at length in the early 1980s with George Bidwell and other Pottery managers who are no longer living. She mentioned that Mr. Bidwell was tireless in his efforts to develop answers to her questions and even took the initiative to provide additional data not requested as well as encouragement and good humor. In listening to some of the old-timers around Abingdon talk appreciatively of Mr. Bidwell and Mr. John Lewis, I regret that I was not able to meet with and talk to them myself.

Don King, a dealer and collector from the Minneapolis area, also sent me a manuscript that he had started. He spent time on the phone talking to me about various aspects of Abingdon pottery. His generosity and good will are appreciated.

Nicol Knappen, former editor of the *Journal of the American Art Pottery Association* and current editor of the *Redwing Pottery Collector's Society Newsletter*, reviewed my manuscript and made many constructive and useful suggestions. Joyce Roerig, a nationally recognized authority on cookie jars and author of several books, provided leads during my early research and was quite generous with her time. Burdell Hall, author of two books on Morton Potteries, which was located in Morton, Illinois, provided input via correspondence and telephone.

Mike Schneider, author of no less than ten books on collecting, provided an introduction to Peter Schiffer which led to this book writing project. In addition, Mr. Schneider provided input not only on my manuscript but on administrative aspects of putting a book together. Thanks should also go to Peter Schiffer for his patience and support in my efforts.

Tom Foley of Midwest Photo Laboratories, Galesburg, Illinois, was helpful in producing reproductions of black and white photographs and in photographing rare pieces that I was not able to access. In Arlington, Virginia, two photo studios were especially helpful in satisfying my very particular concerns for photo developing: 1) Bailey's Epic, owned by Rob and Francine Cannon (Todd Bennett was exceptionally responsive to my requests); and 2) Photo Scope Studios whose owner, Tony Awad, has also been accommodating in providing quality developing and color correction on extremely short notice.

Before paying tribute to the most important contributor of all, I need to point out that I am continually thinking of people who helped me and I am continually revising this section to include them. I know that after the manuscript is sent to the publisher, I will think of someone who should have been included. For those not included here that should have been, please forgive me, the oversight was not intentional.

Now for the Favorite of my life, I need to acknowledge the effort of one constant source of input and support, that of my wife. Without her special skill of putting up with me twenty-four hours a day for the last twenty-five years, this book would never have gotten past the first paragraph. Thanks Joyce.

When I was growing up in the early 1950s in the small town of Avon, Illinois (population 1,000), I knew nothing of Abingdon Pottery artware. I knew that there was a town of Abingdon ten miles to the north on Illinois Route 41 and that there was a pottery there, known by the local population simply as "The Pottery." But as far as I knew, it was a pottery that made plumbing fixtures, as it had since 1908 (and as it still does today).

The Pottery was (and is) a respected institution in the surrounding communities. Many families in the Abingdon area had someone on the payroll at one time or another. Indeed, many families had several members working there, often with decades of service. The work was hard because of the intense heat and because of the strenuous nature of most of the jobs. There was no endless carping nor lack of concern for quality. If you did not make production or if your production did not make muster, you did not continue to work there.

My dad worked there in the late 1950s—a few short years from 1950, the year artware production was discontinued. I remember Dad coming home with chalky salt deposits on his face, clay dust on his clothes, and a yellow sponge head-band on his brow to keep the sweat from his eyes. I remember his arms, face, and neck being "brown as a berry" (even in winter) from direct exposure to the intense heat of the kilns.

When I was a pre-adolescent, my father took me to work to show me what he did. He was a "Placer," someone who placed unfired clay pieces ("greenware") on a rail car which, once loaded, was pushed into the kiln. The hissing of the flames inside the kiln and the intense heat worked on a young boy's fertile imagination. I was terrified and looked up at my dad. His smile of amusement at my emotions is a source of reassurance to me to this day.

I was to experience that heat on a regular basis when I began working there in the late 1960s. I had the job my father had as a Placer. The awesome power of the furnace was still there, performing magic: transforming unfired glazes in velvet-textured pastels into gleaming bright colored porcelain.

Figure AN-1 shows the kiln area. Note the kiln car loaded with sanitaryware. Both dad and I loaded those cars with greenware before they went into the kilns. In

Figure AN-1
The kiln area. *Courtesy of Audrey Sherman.*

Figure AN-2, Thurston Alexander is checking the burners inside the kiln. With colored ware, a change in temperature means a change in color. This inspection became especially important with artware. In Figure AN-3, Ellis Hull pulls the fired pieces from the kiln. Figure AN-4 shows a spray booth where greenware is glazed. This same equipment and the same basic processes were used to make artware. In Figure AN-5, three decorators are applying decorations to artware.

Figure AN-2
Courtesy of Audrey Sherman.

Figure AN-3
Courtesy of Audrey Sherman.

Figure AN-4
Courtesy of Audrey Sherman.

Figure AN-5
Decorators of the
Abingdon Art
Pottery in 1944.
Pictured from left
to right—Doris
Kilpatrick, Bernice
McMillan, and
Arlene Cobb.
Hand painting on
all Abingdon
artware was very
high in quality.
*Courtesy of Rena
London.*

In watching co-workers in the late 1960s, I was struck by the amount of attention and skill used to cast and finish such a lowly item as a piece of plumbingware. Today, when antique dealers and collectors tell me that they are impressed by the quality of the Abingdon artware, I believe it. If extraordinary care was given to plumbingware in the 1960s, it is only logical that at least equal care would have been given to artware in the 1930s and 40s.

I bought my first piece of Abingdon Pottery at an estate sale. I planned to tease my wife by telling her that I worked in the pottery that made the piece—thinking all the while that the "Abingdon, USA" stamped on the bottom was somewhere other than Abingdon, Illinois. To learn where this particular Abingdon actually was, I began to research the subject. I found a book called, Art Pottery of America, by Lucile Henzke, published by Schiffer Publishing, Ltd. Right there in Chapter 1, big as life, was the title, Abingdon Pottery. I quickly learned that it was, indeed, Abingdon, Illinois. What could I do? I turned to my wife and said, "See, I told ya."

Beginning research in earnest, I was surprised to learn that little had been published about Abingdon Pottery artware, Mrs. Lucile Henzke's chapter in her anthology being the most substantive publication. Two other works were published during the early 1980s which deal with The Pottery. One was a chapter in another book on American pottery titled The Dictionary Guide to United States Pottery & Porcelain (19th and 20th Century) written by Dr. Mary Latos and Jenny B. Derwich. The other work was a pamphlet-sized book titled Abingdon Pottery written by Norma Rehl.

Several sources were used continuously in the writing of this book. By far the largest single body of information used was the collection of artware catalogs produced by the Abingdon Pottery during the artware era (1934 to 1950). They numbered more than twenty separate publications and were sent to retailers to advertise what artware pieces were available. The second source of material was the manuscripts and notes developed by John M. Lewis, President of the Abingdon Pottery from 1948 to 1966. The third source of material was a scrapbook developed by Jessie Palmer-Wright, an office employee of the Pottery during the artware era. Finally, the valuable manuscript of Rena London provided research that I was unable to conduct.

Research material aside, nothing speaks better about Abingdon Pottery artware than the artware itself. My wife and I saw our first serious collection of Abingdon when we visited the home of Brian and Anita Hickok. We both marveled at the beauty of the colors, the richness of the glazes, the variety of styling, and the quality of the hand painting. After seeing so many pieces of individual merit, I was convinced that Abingdon Pottery artware represented a contribution to the decorative arts worthy of note. Without seeing a large collection where the various colors, designs, and styling can be viewed together, it is difficult to get a proper appreciation of this body of artware.

This book is designed to introduce Abingdon artware to those who have neither the means nor past experience of viewing a large collection. I have included a significant amount of history and technical detail because I feel the history and the production process of Abingdon, like the artware itself, is unique and worthy of note. One final point.

I am a True Believer when it comes to Abingdon pottery. Some of the earlier drafts of this book were strong in their praise of Abingdon's artistic merit, particularly the glazes. I was cautioned to tone down such praise by several people scholastically well-grounded in the field of American art pottery. They pointed out that Abingdon was an "industrial" pottery, that its glazes were not as world-famous as those of Fulper, Rookwood, and Roseville, and that Abingdon did not hire a large number of artists (some with international reputations it was further pointed out) who spent considerable time experimenting with glazes.

I must admit that Abingdon did not hire a colony of internationally known artists, although the accomplishments of Frances and Leslie Moody did acquire a certain respect, even from some of those artists of international reputation. Abingdon was, indeed, an industrial plant. Its glazes are not as celebrated as those of Rookwood and Fulper. All this is true.

Abingdon's management and personnel were more concerned with surviving the hardships of the Great Depression than they were with competing with Rookwood or Fulper. It was the ingenuity of the Yank (who ever heard of turning plumbingware into artware?) and the artisanship and commitment of the Immigrant as much as formal training that made Abingdon artware what it is—whatever "it" is. It was Huck Finn and Angelo against the Great Depression and Huck and Andy won.

Did these two make art in addition to a living? Hopefully, the information in this book will provide enough data for each reader to make his or her own determination about the technical and artistic merits of Abingdon artware. You be the judge.

LETTER FROM VICE ADMIRAL JAMES B. STOCKDALE, USN (RET)

February 8, 1996
For Joe Paradis, from Vice Admiral Jim Stockdale, USN (ret)

Dear Joe:

I read your manuscript last night and I think it is a fine piece of work—particularly with regard to technical details, thanks probably to John Lewis and his manuscripts. My problem is that, somewhere along the line in this popular rush to acquire Abingdon Pottery artware, my Dad's name was left completely out of the literature. He was Chairman of the Artware Division throughout the whole period—from 1934 through 1950. I really want to set the record straight on this matter. The 1934 to 1950 period accounts for only 15 of my dad's 45 years with the company. Let me give you the history.

V. B. Stockdale was born in Mount Pleasant, Iowa, in 1888 and moved to Abingdon with his parents as a high school boy. James Simpson, an English potter who married an Abingdon-area farm girl he met while she was touring England, decided early in the century to start a pottery in the town of Abingdon both because it was in his wife's native territory and because it was so well serviced by railroads. He stopped en route in Newcastle, Pennsylvania, where a vitreous china factory was located, to hire some of their Italian artisans, who hopefully would be willing to come west to Abingdon for a new start and would teach the Abingdon area natives their skills in the process. Many Italian families migrated to Abingdon and made an outstanding contribution to the success of The Pottery. When Jim finally reached Abingdon, Dad was one of the first people hired. Dad was 19 or 20 when he came on the payroll. When the South Plant opened, it was he who issued the pay cards to the initial hirees.

My Dad was 29 and had been with the company for 10 years when the United States entered World War I. Dad, who was already "white collar," asked for a leave of absence because he wanted to enlist in the U.S. Navy. Jim gave him that and plugged him right back into his job when the war was over. And Dad's service in the Navy in World War I had a lot to do with my life, because Dad had set his heart on my attending Annapolis

and made it happen. I had 37 wonderful years on active duty.

I knew Jim Simpson well. I'm named for Jim Simpson. As Jim Simpson grew prosperous, he hunted in Colorado and later spent winters with Mrs. Simpson in a home they bought in Arizona. Jim retired in 1933 and was replaced as President by Raymond Bidwell, as you mentioned in your text.

Mr. Bidwell had the business sense to use the production capacity for artware to take up the slack left by poor markets for new bathroom ware when construction bottomed out in the Depression. I knew Mr. and Mrs. Bidwell and their two daughters very well, the

Figure AS-1
Vernon B. Stockdale. Started with Abingdon Sanitary Mfg. Company in 1908 as a timekeeper and retired as Vice President in 1953. *Courtesy of Vice Admiral James B. Stockdale, USN (ret)*

younger one of which married John Lewis, my old neighbor whom I always looked up to as an Abingdon High School and Knox College athlete and scholar.

Dad would take my mother and me to The Pottery's "White Elephant" (its real name) Feldspar mine in the Black Hills in the summers of the early 1930s. We got to know the superintendent and all the miners. Mother would collect colorful rocks for her rock garden and the miners would build heavy-duty wooden boxes for them and put them in the rail cars full of feldspar destined to stop at the Abingdon siding of the CB & Q Railroad.

When Dad took over the Artware Division, he traveled a lot setting up pottery sales schemes. I remember that at Marshall Fields in Chicago, in their artware shop were sales personnel whose salaries were partially paid for by the Abingdon Pottery. They were very loyal to my father and the scheme worked well.

Back at the plant, Jessie Palmer-Wright was his very capable assistant and a family friend. Lloyd Petrie had his complete confidence and trust as an experienced man in ceramics. It was Lloyd who helped make some of Abingdon's famed colors and he also helped develop a unique formula for the clay so that it could be molded into the finer shapes that artware required. And, of course, I knew Ralph "Brick" Nelson and his modelers, Joe Pica and Harley Stegall. The contribution of these three should be noted.

When a design was decided upon, the practical world had to be dealt with. It was this trio that took the theory and made a mold that would work. Often, adjustments would have to be made to the designer's ideas to ensure that the cast piece was not broken when taken from the mold. Without their input and cooperation and expertise, many of the designs of the talented design staff would have come to naught. I remember Brick was about 6'3" tall, with brick red hair, and pitched on The Pottery softball team when they played games in the Abingdon Civic League on the old Military School athletic field by the Minneapolis and Saint Louis Railroad tracks just west of the North Plant.

The Moody couple—Leslie and Frances—lived on the same street where I grew up. They later had a couple of daughters that were much younger than I was. I think Dad was responsible for talking Mr. and Mrs. Moody into coming to Abingdon from Ohio. Les was my Scoutmaster, and his wife, Frances, probably had more to do with putting Abingdon artware on the map than anybody. She designed those beautiful sculptured statues. Here in my office, I still have her Cossack Dancer bookends.

After the Artware Division closed, Dad remained as Vice President of the Abingdon Potteries until they were bought by Briggs Manufacturing Company. By that time, Jim Simpson had died. Just before the Briggs sale was announced, Jim's wife, Edith, called Dad from Arizona and said she didn't know what to do with her almost worthless Abingdon Potteries stock. My mother told me this story: Dad knew the Briggs deal was sealed, and that The Pottery stock would immediately make a big jump in price when the sale was announced. When Edith asked Dad if he would please take that stock off her hands, Dad replied: "No, Edith, you hold on to that stock for a while, you'll be glad you did." That is probably my favorite story about the honesty of my dear old Dad—how Dad looked out for the wife of the man who gave him his big chance in life, and gave me my name.

Thanks for giving me the opportunity to input into the history of The Pottery, a history that means so much to me.

—Jim Stockdale

Vice Admiral James Bond Stockdale is a senior research fellow at the Hoover Institution who served on active duty in the regular navy for thirty-seven years, most of those years at sea as a fighter pilot aboard aircraft carriers. Shot down on his second combat tour over North Vietnam, he was a prisoner of war in Hanoi for eight years.

As a civilian, Stockdale has been a college professor and college president and is now in his fourteenth year as a senior research fellow at the Hoover Institution on War, Revolution and Peace. He has written three books while at Hoover: *Thoughts of a Philosophical Fighter Pilot* (1995, forthcoming); *A Vietnam Experience: Ten Years of Reflection* (Hoover Institution Press); and *In Love and War* (Harper and Row, 1984) co-authored with his wife, Sybil, and now in its second revised and updated edition (U.S. Naval Institute Press, 1990).

In 1992, Admiral Stockdale was an independent candidate for Vice President of the United States as the running mate of Ross Perot. In 1993, he was inducted into the Navy's Carrier Aviation Hall of Fame. He holds eleven honorary doctoral degrees.

A VISIT WITH FRANCES MOODY

Figure FM-1
Mrs. Frances Moody with some of her creations in the background.

projects at the Ohio State University in Columbus, Ohio. She titled it "Night." It was in red clay with a flat black glaze (FM-2).

Figure FM-2
The "Mystery Lady" as it had been dubbed by Abingdon Pottery collectors, because it turned up in Jessie Palmer Wright's scrapbook. It was considered a mystery because it never appeared in any of the catalogs and no collector had ever seen it. Mrs. Moody designed this as an undergraduate at Ohio State. As Jessie Palmer Wright's scrapbook indicates, it was fired by Abingdon in white glaze and was among the first pieces displayed at the grand opening of the Artware Division in August of 1934.

For those familiar with Abingdon Pottery Lore, Mrs. Frances Moody is something of an icon. She is the designer of many of the most prized pieces of Abingdon Pottery artware and the wife of Mr. H. Leslie Moody, one of the early managers of the Artware Division that began operation in 1934. Frances Moody, an accomplished sculptress, designed all five sculptured figures sold by the Abingdon Pottery from 1934 to 1938 and a sixth sculpture that was never advertised in the catalogs—the "Mystery Lady" sculpture that is found in pictures taken in August of 1934 at the grand opening of the Artware Division.

I talked to Mrs. Moody several times by phone and corresponded as many times in preparation for our meeting in February, 1996. Upon entering her home, the first thing I noticed was the Mystery Lady. Mrs. Moody explained that it was one of her undergraduate

Frances Moody received a Bachelor's Degree in English from Ohio State University and a Master's Degree in 1929 in Scuplture from the same institution. Leslie Moody also received a Bachelor's Degree in Ceramic Arts from Ohio State. They moved to Dallas, Texas, after college to begin their careers in the ceramic industry. I asked Mrs. Moody to explain the role that she and her husband played in the development of Abingdon artware and how they came to work at the Abingdon Pottery. Mrs. Moody began with a brief biographical sketch of her husband.

H. Leslie Moody was educated and trained in the field of ceramic art at Ohio State University, Columbus, Ohio, where he earned the degree of BFA in CA (Bachelor of Fine Arts in Ceramic Art). He studied under Arthur E. Baggs, who was hired away from Cowan Pottery to develop a course for OSU in all phases of art pottery production. A native of Zanesville, Ohio, and growing up in that central area of the state where good clays were found which encouraged the development of potteries, it seemed only natural that Leslie Moody would find his life's work in the field of art pottery.

During his high school and college years, he found summer employment at many of the potteries of that area. As a college student at OSU, he helped set up the equipment for the newly established Department of Ceramic Art—he learned a lot in this endeavor. The year was 1931 and jobs in those Depression years were very hard to get and those were Depression years. Even though the Crash was 1929, the Depression lasted for a long time. I think it was 1941 before it really recovered.

My husband secured a job at a small pottery in Dallas, Texas, named Love Field Pottery which was very simple production. That pottery also fell to the ravages of the Depression. When my husband told his boss he was going back to Ohio to get married, his boss replied: "Don't get married because the job might not last that long." Well, we got married and moved to Dallas. Of course we did not have anything to move except ourselves and a trunk full of clothes and that was it.

One month after we got there and were settling down nicely, my husband came home one day and said that the job was ending. That was a little unsettling. My husband said to the boss, "If you can't sell your pottery, will you let me go on the road and see if I can sell it?" So, the whole next year, we traveled over the state of Texas, selling mostly crocks and jars of enormous capacity. These big grey jars that grocers stored things in, they stored pickles and such—people were buying them to make home brew.

We shipped a lot of these crocks from that place. But, still the Depression kept struggling on. We were making enough to afford to stay in what was called at that time "tourist courts." And that set up was not doing us very much good. So we decided to return to Columbus, Ohio, where my husband got a job at Ohio State University as an Assistant at the Ceramic Art Department and I began teaching classes to children in sculpture.

It was early after the new year of 1934 when Vernon Stockdale came to Ohio State University looking for a person who could manage an artware division of the master pottery at Abingdon. I can remember seeing Mr. Stockdale, my memory is vivid. I was working in a basement studio equipped for sculpture and ceramic work. When he came in, he was very impressive to me. He was not a tall big man, but there was something about him that was impressive. This was Mr. Vernon B. Stockdale, where the "B" stood for "Beard," a prominent family in the Abingdon area. I kept up a correspondence with his son Jim Stockdale and his wife for a long time and I lost track of them somewhere in California. You know he was on the Perot ticket as Vice-President. Jim was a nice little boy when I knew him back then. He developed into an ace in flying and his commissions in the Navy went up and up and up.

When my husband and I went to Abingdon on our first visit, my husband went to the Pottery and had his interview with Mr. Raymond Bidwell. He came home and we had lunch and Mr. Bidwell asked that I come for an interview in the afternoon, because he was interested in the artistic side of it and wanted to know what I might add. I was asked to be a sort of non-commissioned participant in the program and whenever they wanted something done that was a thing of modeling, I was asked to do it unless someone else in the plant came up with an idea—or even when someone else from the outside presented an idea. Some of the people who worked in the plant had a good artistic comprehension.

My husband and I did most of the designing after the death of Mr. Eric Hertslet. However, my husband had a specialty in glazes. He researched glazes as part of his degree. At one time I had a thick notebook were he kept all his notes on his studies in researching glazes. He was very much interested in glazes as well as the design of the pieces. So, we ended up in Abingdon for eight years and that was a wonderful bit of good luck for us to be connected with Abingdon.

By 1941, business was beginning to pick up at Abingdon and we thought it was a good time for us to break away and pursue our dream of opening our own pottery. After we left Abingdon, we were scouting for our location and came to North Carolina. We did not want a two-man shop but a large pottery with large production capacity. At this time, a ruling from the government said that no new manufacturing processes could be started that used fuel oil. It was the war years and all of the sudden that knocked all our plans to a quick finish. So we began working in the schools in

14

North Carolina when a management job was offered to my husband concerning a pottery in San Antonio, Texas.

The pottery was the San Jose Pottery. It was an open-air shop because it was so warm down there that you could work all year round in the open. The product was red ware. From there the time came when we decided that we were really going to do it and begin our own pottery. The war was over by then and the restrictions on the use of fuel oil were no longer in effect.

We found a lot of interest in Hickory, North Carolina, were we set up our pottery in 1946. Each of our previous experiences gave us valuable knowledge on how to manage a pottery. My husband designed the pottery building as he had two years of architecture before going into ceramics.

I had always been intrigued by the logo "hyalyn" with its unique script and its all lower case, so I asked her how they came up with the name for their pottery.

So, all this time we were thinking about what to call our pottery. We went through art books, pottery books and other books to get ideas. We finally stumbled on a word in a dictionary called hyaline, h-y-a-l-i-n-e. The definition was "a translucent glass-like substance." That fit our definition of pottery completely. To make the word more artistic we changed the name by replacing the "i" with a "y" and by dropping the "e" on the end.

On returning to the subject of Abingdon Pottery artware, I wanted to know what pieces she designed. I asked about the very early pieces (see sketch in Figure 1.5-8a) which had a definite Chinese and Classical influence. "I do not know whether Eric Hertslet designed those or my husband designed those. Since these are in the first catalog, I would attribute these works to Mr. Hertslet because the few things he designed before his death were based on classic shapes."

Mrs. Moody then related how she came to the design of the Reclining Colt bookends (FM-3).

I did a couple of things that were based on my observances in the community. Going North from Abingdon on Illinois Route 41, there is a good-sized curve leading into the straight-a-way to Galesburg. On many of my trips to Galesburg in 1934, I observed a foal lying next to the fence near this large curve. This little foal would be lying out in the pasture in a reclining position with its back legs stretched forward and its front legs bent under, just like the figure in the bookend. I just fell in love with that foal and designed the piece based on that observance.

I had brought more than 1,500 photographs of Abingdon Pottery for Mrs. Moody to review. Mrs. Moody went through the photos and made observations and comments as pictures triggered her memory. She did say that she designed four cookie jars and that "Abingdon went wild with cookie jars after the success of the first cookie jar." The first jar was offered for sale in 1939 and was titled "Little Ol' Lady." She most definitely remembered making that jar and the jar called "Hippo," but could not recall the other two jars. She said that she designed them at her kitchen breakfast table and that the Hippo was especially fun to make.

When Mrs. Moody saw a picture of the Geshia and Coolie tea tiles, she asked several questions to make sure that they were indeed Abingdon creations. Then she said, "The reason I asked is that these are very like tiles that were made at a pottery after we left Abingdon." Mrs. Moody looked at the tea tiles again and said, "I think. I did these."

Figure FM-3
363/Bookend/Reclining Colt/6H/1935-38. Extremely rare. *Courtesy of Robert Rush.*

I showed her a picture of the Kneeling Nude (FM-4) and asked her about that piece. "That also was something I made at Ohio State; I made this piece as a graduate student. I would often go into the sculpture studio and play around with the clay and I'd get an idea and then go for it. And this was one of the things that I liked very much that I did."

The following have been identified by Mrs. Moody as her creations: two wall masks (she believed two smaller masks were adaptations of her work); the Horsehead bookends; the Pouter Pidgeon; the Peacock; the Daisy line of bowls, candlesticks and wall pockets; the Morning Glory and the Double Morning Glory wall pocket; the Little Dutch Boy and Little Dutch Girl. "I made several little birds. The Sea Gull Bookends are mine and the Upright and Leaning goose are mine." She was definite that her husband had designed the Fern Leaf pattern of artware.

Figure FM-4
3903/Sculpture/Kneeling Nude/7H/1935-37. This piece with the green verdigris glaze was one of the pieces done at Ohio State. It is in red clay and has Mrs. Moody's signature. Abingdon fired identical pieces in Antique White, Autumn Peach, Blonde, and Gunmetal Black glazes.

Mrs. Moody designed the elephant and donkey figures that appeared on two ash trays designed for 1940 Presidential election. I mentioned to her that I was told that the elephant and the donkey ash trays came in two sizes. The original became so popular that it was re-issued after the 1940 election in a different size. Her response to this: "I do not know about the difference in size. All I know is that it was an election year and I was to design an elephant and a donkey." It appears that the two fig-ures were then placed not only on ashtrays but two types of boxes, a rectangular cigarette box and a humidor (FM-5).

Concerning the two head vases 3801 and 3802, Mrs. Moody had this to say: "My memory is that a couple of girls came to the pottery wanting to have these things put into clay. I am not sure whether they brought the clay or some kind of a model. I know that they brought it worked up in some way and maybe the pottery then had to make a cast of their original design."

I learned that the chess pieces were another of her college projects and that Hyalyn also did a firing of these pieces. She explained it this way:

I had a desire to re-do these pieces as they suffered a little bit from the molds. Hyalyn ran a firing from these pieces at one time. The chess pieces were another hangover from my college days. A mutual friend of my husband and me that we double dated with came to me and said: "If you will model a double chess set so that we have a set that is playable, I will make the molds and fire them and we will try to market them." That is where the story comes from in the porcelain price books that these pieces were marketed to finance college expenses. One student and I went together to sell one set of chess pieces during my college years. It was bought by a very prominent landscape decorator from New York. The name of the gallery where we sold it was the Arden Gallery. "

The above are recollections of happenings from fifty-five to sixty-two years ago. Mrs. Moody is a most remarkable person. Her gentle manner, her unique phrasing and use of language, her endearing sense of humor, her enthusiasm and joy in pursuing those things in life not yet discovered, left me in a wonder. Mrs. Moody said that she wanted to live to see the new millennium. May God grant that blessing.

Figure FM-5
Smoking accessories designed for the 1940 presidential election.

LETTER FROM M. L. "BUD" CRUMBAKER

5/22/96

Joe

Nice Job. I can see you have done a lot of research. Don't know that I can add much, except anecdotes. I started with the Abingdon Pottery in June of 1934 (my father was an officer of the company and was with them from 1918 until his death in 1939; his name: Erwin W. Crumbaker). My first job was as the first employee in the Artware Inspection, Packing and Shipping Department, right next to Lloyd Petrie's glaze lab. Pete was in charge of all the company's glazes, sanitaryware and artware. His dad (O.M. Petrie) was the local M & St. L. Depot agent at the time. Also, John Lewis's dad was a local barber (Ralph Lewis). To me, Pete and John were just a couple of local guys I grew up with.

I worked under Les Moody as he was the Artware Manager. In fact, when he opened Hyalyn Porcelain Co. in Hickory, after the war, I wanted to leave the old home town, and was the first employee for him. Had an apartment upstairs in the Moody home. His family, Ed Littlefield's family and mine spent a lot of week-ends in the mountains nearby. Sorry, I digressed.

Being new in the artware business there were mistakes made. One time the glaze couldn't take so much heat and ran off, around the bottom. We cut our hands handling it and threw most of it away. Also, one of the orange colors had uranium in the mixture and, when fired, it came out with beautiful black iridescent blotches. We culled the ware. I sure wish I had bought some of that. During the War, we had to ship all the bags of uranium powder to the government. Didn't know then.

Other than nitty gritty artware items, we also made many custom lamp bases for some Chicago lamp manufacturers. Rembrandt Lamp Co. is all I remember.

I was with the company for 12 years. Progressed from artware shipping to plant production office, to the main office, to Shipping Dock Foremen during the war, to Assistant to the Superintendent (Walter Hatch). One of my jobs in the production office—which is of no concern to your Abingdon History—had to do with signing-up and typing the cards for all employees for Social Security (my own, my father's and my sister's were all in numerical sequence). However, the challenging part was getting the correct names and places of birth of the native Italians. The Italians were all good, hard-working people. I went to school with their children. If the kids were working and living at home, the wages went to the family and they got allowances from it. I think all the parents owned their own homes (and others too, often).

You mention Harley Stegall. An incident regarding him: during the Depression, when the plants were shut down, the company wanted to keep key employees so the Foremen and technical people, including the mold makers, were asked to go to the South Plant to start cleaning it up. They were paid $1.00 per day for 10 hours work. Harley was having a hard time keeping his mortgage paid up and asked to get off a half hour early on Saturday (the banks were open until 5 on Saturday). He did get the arrangements made and the next payday his pay was deducted by 5 cents for the half hour he missed. This is a true story.

When I started in 1934, I was paid 23 cents per hour. After 9 months I got a raise to 35 cents, but everyone else was cut from 40 cents to 35 cents.

By the way, did Jim Stockdale tell you he worked in the sagger shop one summer, that Audrey Sherman's father was the Sanding Room Foreman, that she and I worked together in the office? Also, during the War, John Lewis, myself, and two other men went back at night and unloaded feldspar from boxcars for overtime of $1.00 per hour. I see this note is getting a little out of hand, the more I write the more I remember.

Anyway, I left Abingdon in 1946 to go to Hickory with the Moodys. Helped build the plant and was to be in charge of production but after the first few weeks of production was promoted to Plant Superintendent and held that job until the summer of 1954, when I came to Florida.

Although Abingdon is my home town (I'm going back next month to my High School's 62nd class reunion), I also feel very warm about Hickory, N.C. That's a very progressive town. I was back there last month.

Don't know that I've told you anything worth putting in the book, perhaps you have a better feeling and insight in the article you are writing about.

A little about me: I am 80 years old, a widower, lost my wife of 53 years 2 years ago and miss her very much. Have a daughter nearby. Am in good health, square dance 3 times a week and travel a little—not enough.

Sorry about the hand writing. Good luck with the book. Will return the copy you sent.

Sincerely,
M.L. "Bud" Crumbaker.

Figure BC-1
The kiln gang in August 1935, Yanks and Immigrants alike. Front row, left to right: Tom Garrison, Mike Rescinito, Jeff Lawson, Louis Palmiro, Frank Donato, Antonio Marenza, and ??. Second row, Jim Wynkoop, George Amos, ??, Harley Lee, ??, ??, Clyde Peterson, ??. As is mentioned throughout the book, the artisanship and industry of the immigrants from Italy contributed mightily to the success of the pottery and to the rich Abingdon Lore that encompasses events of the entire town, not just the Pottery. Angelo Ippolito and Angelo Mangeiri became Charlie Morey and Andy Martin until names could be properly learned by the Yanks. Other names that trip from the tongue in musical fashion: Arsenio Buzzacaci, Juliani, Guidano, and Francis Lambrosia, Lorenzo Coryo. Other family names populating Abingon's Little Italy: Sabetti, Lamberti, Amato, De Luca, Peluso, Faralli, Pica. Abingdon Lore has it that Arsenio Buzzacaci came to work sick after dressing and eating an Owl. His complaint was that he was "senk in the bell because I ate too much of the big-eyed chick."

1. INTRODUCTION

1.1 PRIMER FOR COLLECTORS AND DEALERS

This section is designed to provide the basic information needed to buy, sell, and collect intelligently. Nearly all Abingdon Pottery artware is worth collecting but, naturally, some pieces are more sought after than others. Therefore, consider giving special attention to:

1. All sculptured pieces;
2. Most early pieces (mold numbers in 300 series);
3. All cookie jars;
4. All pieces in premium colors (see Chapter 3: The Colors);
5. All hand-painted pieces (see Chapter 4: The Decorations);
6. All animal figures, bookends, wall pockets, and kitchen ware;
7. All garden, solarium, sand jars, and floor vases;
8. All Fern Leaf pieces;
9. Pre-artware era art pieces and novelties;
10. Any piece that strikes your fancy.

If the above list sounds like nearly everything, consider this: John Lewis, President of Abingdon Potteries from 1948 to 1966, estimated that 1,000 individual designs were developed with nearly 6,000,000 pieces being sold from 1934 to 1950. Those designs fell into a large number of categories: statues; wall decorations (masks, brackets, and pockets); head vases; chess pieces; animal figurines; animal-shaped planters; book ends; console bowls; candle holders; cornucopias; cigarette accessories; cookie, candy and vanity jars; hors d'oeuvres plates; compotes; cool-drink pitchers; refrigerator containers; range sets; tea sets; tea pot tiles; jam sets; service plates; salad plates; salad and soup bowls; chalices; large garden pots and oil jars; floor vases and sand jars; house flower pots; string holders; lamp bases; flower boats; and decorative bowls.

Pieces were first offered in solid colors with two-tone color offerings available on a special-order basis as early as 1935. With rare exceptions, the two-tone offerings had one color on the interior and one on the exterior. Very few pieces had colors blended together. The prominent practice was to have the two colors clearly separated. Figure 1.1-1 shows two yellow Daffodil vases where colors are blended alongside five other vases where the colors are separate and distinct.

New color "palettes" were offered every six months which meant colors came and went quite regularly. The "premium colors" make a piece prized merely because of the color and texture of the glaze. Mottled glazes and iridescent glazes were produced but are extremely rare today. Most pieces produced were in a gloss finish, although various matt finishes and semi-gloss finishes are common.

Figure 1.1-1
Two-tone colors—the exception and the rule. The two Daffodil planters are the exception because there is a blending of colors. The other pieces represent the rule where the two colors are clearly separated.

With the exception of the gold-trimmed Grecian Bell Crater Urn (#309) offered in the first catalog, hand painting began in 1942 and continued until 1950. All hand painting was glaze painting that was fired. No "cold painting" was ever done at the Abingdon Pottery. Cold painting is painting done with paint after the body is fired and cooled. Cold painting does not bond well with the body while glaze-fired painting is melded into the body during firing. If you see paint chipped or worn away from the glaze on a body with the shape of an Abingdon mold, rest assured that the decoration was cold painted and was not done by Abingdon personnel.

All hand painting, like the workmanship and materials, at the Abingdon Pottery was of unusually high quality. Some pieces do exist (Lunch Box Specials) that show careless workmanship, but they are rare. The general consensus is that they were either seconds or private endeavors of those working in areas not related to artware who dabbled in artware production but had no training. "They were taken home in lunch pails" is the phrase used by old-timers to explain how many pieces of inferior quality—and some of production quality—got out of the plant.

The Abingdon Pottery did sell "blanks" to outside decorating companies. All decal decorations found on Abingdon bodies were decorated by such outside companies. Sometimes a decal or decal-decorated piece will have an Abingdon stamp on the bottom because blanks were sold with that mark on the bottom. However, if the mold number is different than that of Abingdon, the clay body as well as the decoration was made elsewhere.

1.2 HOW TO IDENTIFY ABINGDON POTTERY
(Marks, Labels, Characteristics)

Abingdon Pottery looks different than most artware because it was made differently. Abingdon used the same process to make artware that it used to make its plumbingware. Thus, one intangible identifying characteristic is the robust appearance created by the "industrial strength" materials and processes used to make the bodies and glazes. Another intangible characteristic is the styling of Abingdon. Recognizing the styling of Abingdon will require training the eye through flea market and antique mall research as well as studying the pictures in this book—which takes time and practice.

However, there are identification characteristics that can be picked up with the untrained eye. For example, look for grinding marks on the base of the piece, as nearly all Abingdon Pottery artware was ground at the base. Some bottoms were glazed and some were not, but all exposed clay should be white, allowing for discoloration due to age and abuse. This exposed clay must be vitreous or non-porous. Vitreous means that the clay was fired at such a high temperature that the clay shrinks, implodes really, about 10 to 12% and, due to this compacting, the body becomes glass-like and will not absorb moisture.

Also, look for a mold number on the bottom of the piece. Some pieces, however, do not have a mold number because: 1) it was inadvertently omitted during production; 2) it was placed on at production but the glaze filled in the impression during firing—this frequently happened with the black gloss glaze; 3) no mold number was ever assigned (it is speculated that they were not production pieces but, rather, experimental pieces that never passed marketing tests).

The oldest pieces have the mold number raised above (embossed on) the surface of the clay. Later pieces have the mold number impressed below the surface of the base. Figure 1.2-1 shows both situations, the raised or embossed mold number found on the dark blue glazed piece to the left and the impressed number is found on the lighter blue base to the right. Figure 1.2-2 shows an unglazed bottom with an impressed mold number. For whatever reason, *Classic* vases and *LaFleur* flower pots along with What Not vases and animal figures had "dry" or unglazed bottoms.

In addition to a mold number, the bottoms of most Abingdon Pottery artware had factory marks in the form of either ink stamps or impressions. Sometimes both were present, i.e., impressions with ink in the bottom of the impression to highlight the impression. Figure 1.2-3 provides examples of the four most commonly used ink stamps (the "A.P.C. 1983" is not an Abingdon factory stamp but a logo used by the Abingdon Pottery Collector's Club for this 1983 banquet memento).

Figure 1.2-1
Raised (embossed) number at left; impressed mold number at right.

Figure 1.2-2
Unglazed bottom of *Classic* vase. Note the white color of the fired clay. All exposed clay should be this color, allowing for discoloration due to abuse and age.

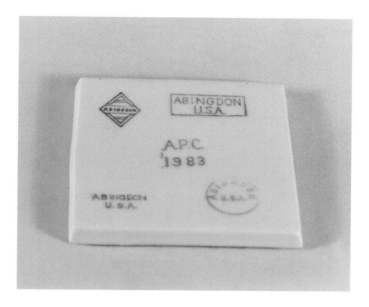

Figure 1.2-3
Four of the most common ink stamps used by Abingdon. The "A.P.C. 1983" in center is for "Abingdon Pottery Club 1983" and dates this banquet memento.

At the top left corner of the tile in Figure 1.2-3 is an example of the oldest ink stamp used by Abingdon. Figure 1.2-4 shows this ink stamp on an early piece with the remnants of the earliest label of the same design. This label is shown intact in Figure 1.2-5. The design of this label and corresponding ink stamp is here dubbed "Double A" to distinguish it from a simpler design called here "Diamond A"—see Figure 1.2-6. This simpler factory mark was also placed on non-artware pieces such as soda fountain jars and sanitaryware.

By far the most common mark used was the large rectangle ink stamp. It was stamped in either blue or black ink—see Figure 1.2-7. Another common ink stamp was the circular ink stamp referred to as the "Postage Stamp" because of its similarity to the validation stamp used by the U. S. Postal Service—see Figure 1.2-8. Another mark resembling

the circular ink stamp was the semi-circle impressed mark shown in Figure 1.2-9. The mark shown in Figure 1.2-10 is both ink stamp and clay impression, with the ink highlighting the impression. Ink highlighted impressions are also shown in Figure 1.2-6 previously discussed. Marks from outside decorating firms sometimes accompanied Abingdon marks—see Figure 1.2-11. This particular outside mark is usually found on pieces with high quality decoration.

While the large rectangle was the most frequently used ink stamp, the most frequently used label is found in Figure 1.2-12. Three versions of this label (metallic gold and yellow, metallic silver, and brown and cream paper) were made—see Figure 1.2-13. The yellow and gold is the most frequently found of the three while the paper label in the center is the oldest of the three.

The *Classic* line was a series of vases and the *LaFleur* line

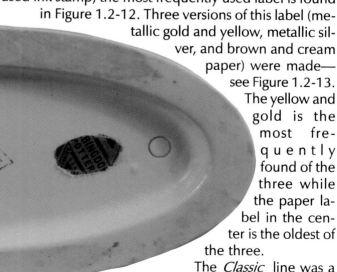

Figure 1.2-4
Double A ink stamp and remnant of paper label of same design—oldest ink stamp and oldest paper label.

line a series of flower pots that first appeared in 1938. Two *Classic* labels are shown in Figures 1.2-14 and 15— a brown paper and a silver metallic label. One *LaFleur* label is found in Figure 1.2-16. This label was issued in blue as shown and black which is not shown. Figure 1.2-17 shows the label that was found on the eight pieces of refrigerator ware issued in 1940.

Figure 1.2-5
Double A label intact. Note the felt on the bottom as Abingdon used dark brown felt on many pieces in the early days.

Figure 1.2-6
Diamond A mark, as opposed to the Double A mark. This mark is impressed into the clay and highlighted by ink. It is also accompanied by the small rectangle ink stamp. The small rectangle ink stamp was often found on smaller pieces and on larger pieces sold as blanks to decorating firms.

Figure 1.2-7
Most commonly found ink stamp. Came in both blue and black ink. Referred to as the large rectangle stamp.

Figure 1.2-8
Referred to as the postage stamp. For whatever reason, early postage stamps on What Not vases would rub off. Later stamps were fired and thus became permanent.

22

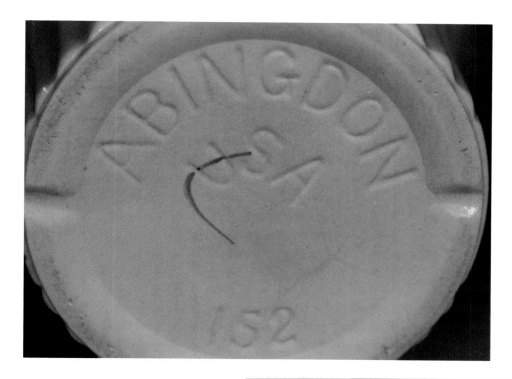

Figure 1.2-9
Referred to as the semi-circle mark. Most often found on *LaFleur* pieces.

Figure 1.2-10
A clay impressed mark highlighted by ink—as are the two pieces shown in Figure 1.2-6 above. This mark is sometimes accompanied by the letters U.S.A. below the word ABINGDON.

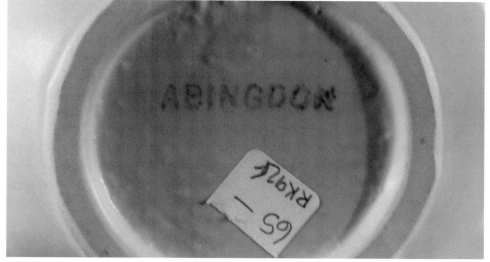

Figure 1.2-11
One of the "blanks" sold to an outside decorating firm—note that the firm's mark accompanies Abingdon's large rectangle ink stamp. The small rectangle more frequently accompanied outside decorator stamps. This mark accompanies the best of the non-Abingdon decorations.

Figure 1.2-12
Most frequently found label.

Figure 1.2-13
Three versions of
the most fre-
quently found
label—metallic
gold, metallic
silver on each
side, and paper in
the middle. Paper
label is the oldest
version.

Figure 1.2-14
Early *Classic* line paper label.

24

Figure 1.2-15
Silver metallic version of *Classic* Line
label.

Figure 1.2-16
Blue *LaFleur* label.
Also came in
black.

Figure 1.2-17
Label used on the eight pieces of
refrigerator ware issued in 1940.

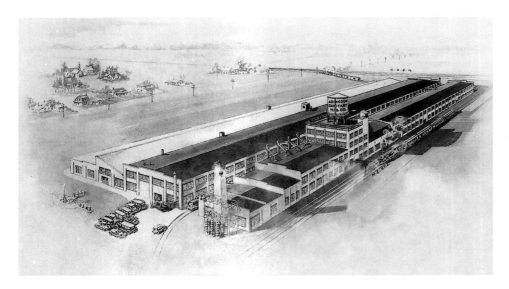

Figure 1.3-1
Abingdon Sanitary Manufacturing
Company North Plant prior to 1939.
Courtesy of Audrey Sherman.

Figure 1.3-2
Movers and Shakers, May 5, 1936, Top
Row Left to Right: Lee Casler, Treasurer;
Raymond E. Bidwell, President; Erwin W.
Crumbaker, Secretary; Edwin Sinn,
Harrison, New Jersey. Bottom Row, Left to
Right: Edwin Stern, Cleveland; Chas.
Schmitz, Chicago; Geo. Wobensmith,
Philadelphia; Ted Brownson, Company
Auditor; Lee Delavigne, Detroit; Emil
Schwerdtle, New York City; Roy Mangum,
Chicago; Vernon Stockdale, Mgr,
Abingdon; Harold Greenman,
Hammondsport, NY; Arthur Joliffe,
Minneapolis; Clyde Woods, Nashville;
Don Stephan, Sales Dept, Abingdon; Les
Moody, Mgr, Abingdon; Walter Hatch, V.P.
in charge of Production; Richard Hanson,
No. Central Mississippi River States.
Courtesy of Audrey Sherman.

Figure 1.3-3
Workers in the Casting Division, August
22, 1935. *Courtesy of Audrey Sherman.*

1.3 HISTORY

Abingdon Pottery artware was produced from 1934 to 1950 by the Artware Division of a small company located in the town of Abingdon, Illinois (population then and now, approximately 3,000). This small company was founded in 1908 as the Abingdon Sanitary Manufacturing Company. This name was changed to Abingdon Potteries, Inc. in 1945. It is now called Briggs Industries, Inc., and still makes plumbing fixtures.

Early in 1934, the Abingdon Pottery secured the services of a talented ceramic engineer (Leslie Moody), a promising designer (Eric Hertslet), and a gifted sculptress (Frances Moody). Abingdon also had a pool of home-grown talent who played a crucial role in the designing of shapes and of colors and glazes (Vernon B. Stockdale, Ralph "Brick" Nelson, George Bidwell, Harley Stegall, Joe Pica, Lloyd Petrie, Arsenio Ippolito, and many others).

Vernon Stockdale, beginning his forty-five-year career at The Pottery as a clerk, retired as a Vice-President of the company in 1953. His contribution was multi-faceted. He had a good managerial sense, a commanding presence, and an affinity for people. It was Mr. Stockdale who scouted the Midwest and acquired the outside talent. It was Mr. Stockdale who ensured that the many immigrant Italian families coming to Abingdon with their Old World expertise were properly acclimated. The talent, effort, and contribution of all the "home-grown" talent mentioned above cannot be overestimated. Many of the designs after January 1, 1941, were the result of the efforts of this local talent, as the Moodys left Abingdon on that date to pursue their goal of opening a pottery of their own.

John M. Lewis, President of Abingdon Potteries, Inc., from 1948 to 1966, developed two manuscripts and other materials which documented the history of this small company and which provided detailed information on how the pottery made its products. Mr. Lewis clearly indicated in these two manuscripts that Abingdon had been a leader in developing porcelain ware. Mr. Lewis pointed out that The Pottery: 1) developed in 1908, a casting process of producing plumbing fixtures, a great improvement over the pressing method used at the time; 2) built the first sagger-type tunnel kiln in the vitreous china plumbing fixture industry in 1920; 3) produced colored plumbing fixtures before most of its competitors; 4) produced all the plumbing fixtures for the World's Fair buildings in Chicago in 1933. Not bad for a small company.

Business was good for the first two decades because of the quality of the merchandise and the expertise of the staff, both management and labor. When the Depression came in 1929, demand for plumbing fixtures dropped continuously over the next four years, causing much of the production capacity to become idle. This situation was remedied by Yankee Ingenuity. What follows are edited excerpts from the works of John M. Lewis.

The idea for Abingdon art pottery was the brainchild of Raymond E. Bidwell, who came to Abingdon as president in 1933 in the depth of the Great Depression. The directors of what was then named the Abingdon Sanitary Manufacturing Company brought him to Abingdon to save the company from possible bankruptcy. He was faced with two vitreous china plumbing fixture manufacturing plants that were shut down. They were at op-

Figure 1.3-4
John M. Lewis, President 1948 to 1966 and official responsible for developing historical manuscripts about Abingdon Pottery artware. *Courtesy of Mrs. John Lewis.*

Figure 1.3-5
Raymond E. Bidwell, President 1933 to 1948 and official responsible for starting artware production at Abingdon. *Courtesy of Mrs. John Lewis.*

posite ends of Abingdon with the South Plant containing 176,000 square feet and the North Plant 174,000. They were far too expensive to keep in operation without additional production and something drastic had to be done. What could the excess capacity be used for?

Mr. Bidwell came up with the idea of making art pottery and distributing it nationally and internationally. It was determined that it could be produced in the same facilities, initially by using the same body, the same kilns, the same glazes, the same colors and the same production methods used in making plumbing fixtures. The vitreous china body is far superior to the usual earthenware or non-vitreous bodies typically used in art pottery so this would have sales appeal. It should immediately be considered a top-of-the-line product.

With a fine china product of distinctive design and limited production, sales were sought in gift shops and department stores. It was felt that a name product was not needed to impress these buyers, as the artware would be sold by the obvious quality and appeal of the pottery.

Glazes of unusual texture were developed because it was thought something other than the conventional sanitaryware and dinnerware glazes would have great appeal. Matt, crystalline, and iridescent glazes were brought out along with the regular gloss, mottled and crazed effects other potteries were using. New or different glazes or colors were brought out about every six months, following the trend of color that was popular for drapes and home furnishings at that time. F. Q. Mason of Mason Color and Chemical Works at East Liverpool, Ohio, helped greatly in the color endeavor with his extensive and unique knowledge of colors and their development.

A great plus was the skill and experience of Lloyd R. Petrie, who was an expert in both bodies and glazes. Mr. Petrie developed a special versatile white vitreous china body for art pottery. With it, fine handles could be cast, and it was also suitable for casting pieces separately and then sticking them together. It proved to be a super body. Had it not been for the endless and unselfish efforts of Pete, the Art Ware Division would have been doomed to an early failure.

Another real plus was the varied experiences of the modelers who were skilled in making the many different designs. Ralph Nelson, who was in charge of the department, had great skill and ingenuity. His knowledge was gained from both U. S. and Italian modelers. Mr. Nelson, Joe Pica, and Harley Stegall, were the key people in the modeling of the more than 1000 different pieces. These modelers were skilled in making adjustments and working out the production problems that were not taken into consideration by the designers.

It is important to give credit here to the great contribution of the Italian families who came to Abingdon when the pottery was started in 1908. Their skill, their conscientious nature, their determination, their sacrifices and their dedication made the difference between success and failure in the early months and years of Abingdon's existence. Without them and their cooperation there might never have been any Abingdon art pottery.

Art pottery production was carried on for a 17-year period from 1934 to 1950 inclusive. The number of employees was 110 (one third of whom were women); the number of colors or shades was 149; the total number of pieces produced was 6,000,000; the sales volume was $3,500,000.

After one section of the plant was vacated for artware production and a new high-speed art pottery tunnel kiln was put into service, distribution was widened by adding customers in mail order and jobbing accounts in the United States and foreign countries. Japanese competition with Abingdon designs came about in 1946-47 when Carson, Pirie, Scott shipped Abingdon artware to the Japanese. Direct copies of this pottery were coming back to the USA. These pieces even had Abingdon's own catalog numbers in reverse on the bottom of the pottery.

Plans for producing and selling a million pieces of artware a year were scheduled to be implemented in 1950. That year, because of heavy demands and strong pressures to produce more vitreous china plumbing fixtures, the major product line of the company, a tough decision faced Abingdon Potteries, Inc. The only apparent way to get more plumbing fixtures fast was to discontinue the artware production and use that space for the production of plumbing fixtures.

On September 16, 1950 announcements were mailed to 2750 customers informing them that artware production would be discontinued but that all orders on hand would be shipped and additional orders postmarked before September 22 would be accepted and filled. As each production step was completed, the department was shut down with the final step, the closing down of the kiln, occurring on November 17, 1950. On this date, production of the prized and distinctive Abingdon china art pottery was concluded. Shipments, however, continued through the end of the year.

Most of the employees were absorbed in sanitaryware production after the dismantling of the kiln and moving out the production equipment. The control instruments, burners, steel cars and special refractories from the kiln were retained for possible future use. Some of the production equipment was sold to Haeger Pottery and other pottery producers. The molds were sold to Pidgeon Vitreous China Company Pottery at Barnhart, Missouri, and were later moved to Western Stoneware of Monmouth, Illinois. Thus, some of the Abingdon designs were continued in production for years. This production, though, was not vitreous china, and some people may have pieces that they think are Abingdon but are not.

For months and years after production stopped, the Abingdon Pottery kept getting inquiries from people who wanted to purchase it. Many were from people who wanted more of the quality pottery they already had. Others were from people who obviously had been reading Better Homes & Gardens magazines, in which Abingdon had advertised extensively.

Thus, a notable contribution to the world of American art pottery came to an end, as it had begun, through a shrewd and profitable business decision.

CHRONOLOGY
OF THE ABINGDON POTTERY
(Based on the Notes of John M. Lewis)

1908 Abingdon Sanitary Manufacturing Company founded.

1912 Railroad car closet production began.

1917 Plumbing fixtures for military war effort (WWI) began.

1920 First sagger-type tunnel kiln in the industry built in Abingdon.

1928 Rights to Feldspar Mines near Custer, South Dakota obtained. Crude feldspar shipped to Abingdon via C. B. & Q. And M. & St. L. Railroads. Feldspar used in the manufacture of plumbing fixtures. Also sold to two other firms.

1928 Production of industry's first colored plumbing fixtures began.

1928 Self-ventilating water closets developed and sold.

1933 R. E. Bidwell replaced James Simpson as President.

1933 All plumbing fixtures for the World's Fair buildings in Chicago made.

1934 Production of art pottery began.

1938 South Plant machinery and equipment sold.

1939 South Plant buildings wrecked. Tunnel kiln built at North Plant for exclusive use of art pottery. An additional 60,000 square feet of floor space built.

1942 Production of plumbingware for military use began.

1945 Art pottery kiln rebuilt and lengthened. Art pottery production expanded. Company name changed from Abingdon Sanitary Manufacturing Company to Abingdon Potteries, Inc.

1946 78,000 square feet additional space built.

1947 Three new tunnel kilns put into operation—much more efficient than the two original kilns which were wrecked. Office building expanded again. On October 15, 1947, controlling stock sold to Briggs Manufacturing Company of Detroit.

1948 J. M. Lewis replaced R. E. Bidwell as President of Abingdon Potteries, Inc.

1950 Art Pottery discontinued to expand on plumbing fixture production.

1951 Art pottery kiln wrecked and space used for plumbingware production; 25,600 square feet added and a new kiln built.

1966 Retirement of J. M. Lewis after 18 years in charge of all corporate, office and manufacturing operations; also, as Corporate Vice-President of Briggs Manufacturing Company in charge of all ceramic manufacturing plants and operations.

Figure 1.4-1
Article of artware era vintage about the progressive nature of the Abingdon Pottery's state-of-the-art production techniques. *Courtesy of Mrs. John Lewis.*

1.4 THE PRODUCTION PROCESS

Again, without the richly detailed account of John Lewis, how the Pottery made its artware would have been lost. This accounting is of value not only to historians, but to those collectors wanting to know as much about their pottery as possible. The following are more edited excerpts from Mr. Lewis's manuscripts.

Abingdon Pottery was made in an environment where painstaking workmanship and dedication to quality were paramount. Specially selected china clays from England and Georgia, ball clays from England and Tennessee, flint and ground silica sand from points in Illinois, and feldspar from mines in the Black Hills of South Dakota all went to make up the body. The feldspar in this mixture, being a fusing material, binds the various clays and flint together under intense heat while the china clays provide fast casting and light color and the ball clays give strength in production and in the finished product.

The ball clays were first carefully weighed and then put through a preliminary washing process in which water was added and the mixture stirred until the complete mass was in a fluid state. This mixture was then passed through vibrating screens which extracted lignite and other undesirable substances which would be detrimental to the body. From the screens it went to a magnetic separator which removed any iron that would appear as specks on the finished product. This ball clay mixture was pumped into a pebble mill which had previously been charged with the exact weights of china clays, flint and feldspar required for the batch. The batch was then milled with additions of electrolytes such as silicate of soda and soda ash until tests proved that it had the desired working properties.

The product of this operation was a smooth liquid clay known in the industry as "slip." It was then ready to again pass to a battery of vibrating screens or lawning machines which took out par-

ticles that were too large or which represented foreign matter that must be removed to assure a good product. The slip was next sent through more magnetic separators which drew out any traces of iron that may have lingered in the clays up to that point, and the slip was then pumped to large tanks where it was stored until it was needed for casting.

Through an elaborate system of pipes, valves and controls, the slip was pumped to the area where it was poured into plaster molds. The plaster molds absorbed the water in the slip and, as a result, the clay solidified next to the plaster. On a drain-cast piece, the desired thickness of clay was obtained by the length of time that the liquid clay remained in the molds and any excess slip was drained out.

The thickness of the solid-cast sections was determined by the molds, but timing was still an important factor. The molds were then taken apart, and in some cases different parts were stuck together, depending upon the type of piece being made, and the unit was ready for the first rough finishing by hand. The final finishing took place after a prolonged drying period during which temperatures and humidity were controlled. The ware was usually sent to be glazed about 3 days after it was cast.

Glaze preparation was, of course, going on at the same time that slip was being made, so that it would be ready when the ware was brought to the sprayers. The ingredients for white glaze were chiefly feldspar, flint, china clay, whiting, barium carbonate, talc, zirconium opacifier and a binder. The colored glazes were basically the same except for the addition of the necessary stains to obtain the proper colors. Water was added and the batches milled until tests showed that the proper characteristics had been reached.

Before the ware went to the sprayers, it was inspected and all pieces that did not meet rigid standards were rejected. Then it passed to the sprayers who first blew it off to make sure that no surface dirt would cause trouble and then proceeded to apply the glaze using a three- or four-coat process to make sure that every surface was properly covered and that there was not too much of a buildup at any one point. If the pieces were to be decorated, colored decorating stains were painted over the glaze.

From spraying and/or decorating, the ware passed on to a point where it was placed on kiln cars and lined up to go into the kiln. The cars moved through the kiln at a predetermined schedule which meant that all pieces were fired under uniform conditions. The extreme temperature to which the clay ware was subjected was 2350 degrees F. One and one half to two days elapsed, depending upon the schedule, from the time the ware entered the kiln until it came out the other end, a vitreous china product. The finished piece was approximately 12 per cent smaller than the original size in the mold.

Firing of art pottery was done in the same 400 foot oil fired Harrop tunnel kilns that fired sanitaryware when the Artware Division was started. The kiln had a width of 5 feet with a height of 7 feet. Ware was placed in saggers to keep the blast of the direct oil fire from striking the pottery. After the ware came from the kiln, it again went through an extremely careful inspection process, this time of a different type as the ware was in its final form. All pieces were looked over for surface defects and to make sure that the colors were right. The bases were ground if necessary.

In 1934, when the artware production began, the standard manufacturing process in the industry was to fire ware twice. One of the kilns was used for firing unglazed or "bisque" ware at a temperature of 2350 degrees F. The other, glost kiln, was for the second firing at 2150 degrees after the glaze was applied. The placing and drawing of the art pottery was a difficult job because the man involved had to lift and replace the heavy refractory saggers each time a piece was fired. It was a striking sight to see the men balance the saggers on their heads when they moved them. Because of the two-fire operation and lack of space in the North Plant, art pottery production was limited.

So, it was decided that one-fire operations would be considered. An experimental one-car kiln was built at the west end of the kiln building. This kiln was used for experimental purposes in connection with developing bodies, glazes, casting methods, placing methods and experimental firing. In 1939, construction was started on a 135-foot Swindell-Dressler indirect fired muffle kiln, which was completed in 1940. From then on, artware was produced on a one-fire basis. With the muffle kiln and one fire, labor costs were cut drastically, there was far more firing capacity and production was greatly expanded.

In this kiln, the pottery was fired in the open on .75 inch thick silicon carbide slabs. Two or more decks were usually used with the upper decks supported by refractory posts. The firing space was 30 inches in width by 30 inches in height. Automatic controls were used to assure uniform firing temperatures.

In 1945 the kiln was lengthened to 185 feet and revisions were made by Harrop which greatly improved the kiln performance and increased its capacity. The Artware Division was also equipped with a Denver Fire Clay decorating kiln, which was used for gold decorating and for other special decorating functions. This kiln seldom was used on a production basis.

The Rena London manuscript contains additional valuable information about the production process. Edited excerpts from her manuscript are provided below:

The clay piece, after being cast in the plaster mold, was removed from the mold, dried, and glazed. The majority of the glazing was done by spraying. The surface glaze was applied with DeVilbiss spray guns in large spray booths. Open-top pieces which were large enough were sprayed inside with the DeVilbiss guns; narrow-necked items such as vases had the glaze pumped into them. The piece was held upside down over the top of a nozzle connected to an air-operated glaze pump set in the middle of a galvanized wash cup filled with glaze. The air-operated pump was activated by a foot switch. Dipping was used for glazing about 20% of the production, mostly smaller items.

After glazing, if the piece was to be decorated, it was transported to the decorating department and all decorations and patterns were applied by hand, using either camel-hair artist brushes or ox-ear hair brushes for finer details. After additional drying, the ware was then placed on the kiln car furniture and sent through the kiln for firing. Being a one-fired piece of ware, the decoration became part of the body glaze which in turn became part of the clay body.

All Abingdon Pottery, with the exception of lamp bases and a few other objects had a footing or grinding edge on the bottom. The artware was placed on silicon carbide furniture slabs on the kiln cars. To keep the ware from sticking to the slabs, a wash of aluminum oxide mixed with a small amount of clay binder was applied.

After firing, the footing would come out with some of the slab wash stuck to it and in order to remove it and dress up the bottom, the pieces were ground off on a converted engine block flat wheel surface, 5.5 inches in diameter powered by a 25 horse power vertical motor, which revolved at 450 RPMs. The grinding surface was one inch thick and made of silicon carbide with free running water used for cooling the surface as well as the ware footing. The body, being vitrified, was very hard and without the water, sparks would fly.

Any green colored Abingdon Pottery was made from a formula using chrome oxide—it is the same material the U.S. Treasury uses to print our currency.

The extremely high gloss solid black and matt black glaze was developed by Lloyd Petrie. Arsenio Ippolito, who worked at the Abingdon Pottery from 1923 to 1936, also was instrumental in developing glazes. He worked with glazes of all colors, but stated that the hardest one to perfect was the black glaze. The difficulty was that it was harder to cover the items as the edges would become transparent. Workers kept changing formulas. It took almost a year to perfect the black glaze.

Abingdon produced over 500,000 lamps. Most of the volume was in ivory or off-white and many of these had a flower, stem and leaf in raised design on one side which, in some instances, was hand-painted. All Abingdon standard colors were produced on lamp bases in solid gloss glaze, but there were no two-tone or other types of effects.

Some lamps were sent to decorator shops and had decals applied and/or other types of decoration (such as gold or silver trim) applied by brushing. Abingdon lamps were sold to brokers and had neither label nor model number. The brokers in turn marketed them through volume sales such as the cigarette premium books published during the war years or sold them to lamp assemblers who mounted the ceramic bases on wood or metal bases.

It is unfortunate, indeed, that personal hardships interrupted Mrs. London's book-writing project. As the valuable passages above indicate, she had made a significant contribution to the scholarship on Abingdon Pottery artware.

1.5 A GALLERY OF COLLECTIBLES

With more than 1,000 individual shapes and decorative variations of many of those shapes, a complete accounting of even the most prized pieces would be as lengthy as it would be subjective. The 1.5 series of figures provides a brief sampling of pieces—prized and otherwise.

Figure 1.5-1a, b, and c
3901/Nescia/16H/1935-37.

Figure 1.5-2
3902/Scarf Dancer/13H/1935-37.

Figure 1.5-3a
3903/Seated Nude/7H/1935-37 in Gunmetal Black.

Figure 1.5-3b
3903/Seated Nude/7H/1935-37 in Antique White and Verdigris; White glaze piece was fired by Abingdon while the Verdigris was fired at Ohio State University when Mrs. Moody was a graduate student (1929).

Figure 1.5-4
3904/Fruit Girl/10H/1937-38 in Blonde glaze. Another Frances Moody creation.

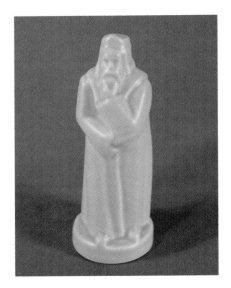

Figure 1.5-5a
3905B/Bishop/4.5H/1937 and 3905Q/Queen/5H/1937.

The chess pieces are extremely rare with no known collection containing them all. The pieces were also fired by Hyalyn Porcelain after the Moodys founded that pottery in Hickory, North Carolina, in 1946.

Figure 1.5-5b
3905K/King/5.5H/1937.

Figure 1.5-5c
3905P/Pawn/3.5H/1937.

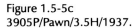

Figure 1.5-6a
3906/Shepherdess & Fawn/11.5H/1937-38 in Autumn Peach with non-Abingdon gold decoration. This decoration violates Fran Moody's belief that "a good design and a good glaze should be able to stand alone." This design was reproduced by Abingdon personnel in the late 1980s and 1990s. The repro has six fingers on the hand touching the fawn. *Courtesy of Knoxville Museum.*

Figure 1.5-7a
3801/Large Head vase/11.5H/1936-38 top view. *Courtesy of Betty Perry. Photo taken by Tom Foley of Midwest Photo.*

Figure 1.5-7b
3801/Large Head vase/11.5H/1936-38 side view. *Courtesy of Betty Perry. Photo taken by Tom Foley of Midwest Photo.*

Figure 1.5-6b
3906/Shepherdess & Fawn/11.5H/1937-38. *Courtesy of Betty Perry. Photo taken by Tom Foley of Midwest Photo.*

Figure 1.5-7c
3801/Large Head vase/11.5H/1936-38 back view. *Courtesy of Betty Perry. Photo taken by Tom Foley of Midwest Photo.*

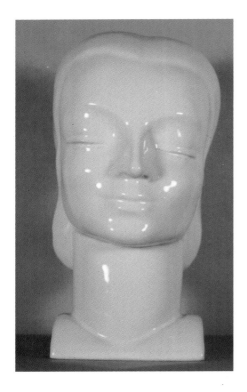

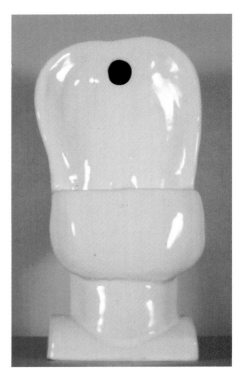

Figure 1.5-8a
3802/Small Head vase/8.5H/1936-38
front view. *Courtesy of Brian and Anita Hickok.*

Figure 1.5-8b
3802/Small Head vase/8.5H/1936-38 side view. *Courtesy of Brian and Anita Hickok.*

Figure 1.5-8c
3802/Small Head vase/8.5H/1936-38
back view. *Courtesy of Brian and Anita Hickok.*

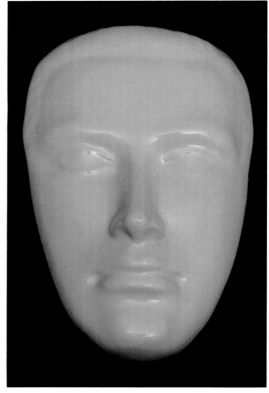

Figure 1.5-9b
376M Large Male Mask/7.5H/1936. Note that 378M is a smaller version of this (4.0H). *Courtesy of Betty Perry. Photo taken by Tom Foley of Midwest Photo.*

Figure 1.5-9a
376F Large Female Mask/7.5H/1936. Note that 378F is a smaller version of this (4.0H). *Courtesy of Christine and Jamie Boone.*

Figure 1.5-10a Artist's sketch of "The Early Pieces" pieces offered in the first two catalogs (Spring 1934 and Fall of 1935). These pieces could also be referred to as the "Hertslet and Moody Collections" as Eric Hertslet and Leslie and Frances Moody are considered the originators of most if not all of these pieces. Those with Chinese and Classical influence are Mr. Hertslet's.

Figure 1.5-10b
Examples of the Early Pieces in Copper Brown. *Courtesy of Christine and Jamie Boone.*

Figure 1.5-10c
Another Early Piece, Ring vase in Lemon Yellow.

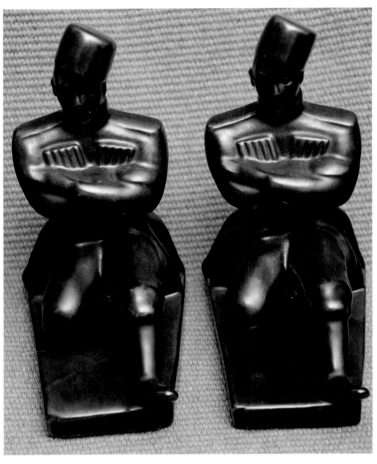

Figure 1.5-10d
Still another Early Piece, set of Russian bookends in Gunmetal Black. *Courtesy of Betty Perry. Photo taken by Tom Foley of Midwest Photo.*

Figure 1.5-10e
Final selection of Early Pieces, Abingdon Square and Round dinnerware. Abingdon made no concerted effort to provide service ware for the table. What developed—with the exception of the pieces shown here and a square soup not shown—was on an ad hoc basis. Refrigerator ware, cool drink pitchers, and various bowls, tea sets, range sets, and vases that could be used as chalices were made but not as a tableware "line." *Courtesy of Robert Rush.*

Figure 1.5-11
Selection of Fern Leaf Pieces.

Figure 1.5-12
Animal figures
from left to right:
hand-painted
Swordfish; hand-
painted Buddha;
Black Pelican;
hand-painted
Kangaroo; Black
Penguin; hand-
painted Little Boy
with Sand Pail;
Ram Planter;
Black Sitting
Goose; hand-
painted Heron.

Figure 1.5-13
Little Dutch Boy and Little Dutch Girl
vases. Wall pockets were also made.

Figure 1.5-14
An assortment of hand painted pieces: vanity, candy, and cigarette boxes. *Courtesy of Robert Rush.*

Figure 1.5-15
Another assortment of hand-painted pieces.

Figure 1.5-16
Royal Blue *Classic* vase 114. Any piece in this "premium" color is sought after. *Courtesy of Christine and Jamie Boone.*

Figure 1.5-17a and b
Six "Fine Handled vases" as they were dubbed in the catalogs. Top Row: Abbey, Acadia and Arden in blue, yellow, and green; Bottom Row: Berne, Barre, and Baden in blue, yellow, and pink. The "A"s are 7 inches and the "B"s are 9 inches.

Figure 1.5-18
Kangaroo, also shown in 1.5-10. This is an extremely rare piece.

Figure 1.5-19
The small Royal Blue vase on the right was given out in August of 1934 to all who attended the grand opening of the Artware Division at the Abingdon Pottery. It is accompanied by a Fire Red Rope vase which is 6 inches high. Both colors are premium colors and sought after. The smaller vase is extremely rare.

Figure 1.5-20
Royal Blue Refrigerator Water Jug, hand-painted Blackamoor bud vase, and Black Trojan Head bookend/vase. *Courtesy of Elaine Westover.*

2. THE NUMBERS

2.1 OVERVIEW

Nearly all production pieces made by Abingdon had a mold number placed on the bottom of the piece. The general rule concerning mold numbers: most are three-digit numbers 101 through 734 with one (861) in the 800 series. The exceptions to this general rule are: two two-digit numbers (98 and 99); eleven four-digit numbers (3801, 3802, 3901-6 with six variations of 3905 for the six pieces of a chess set, 9699, 9700, 9701); and, the following alpha numeric number series: A1 through A6; B1 through B6; C1 through C6; G1 through G4; P4 through P8; and, RE1 through RE8.

2.2 TWO-DIGIT MOLD NUMBERS

| 98 | Animal Figure | Upright Goose | 5H | 1948-50 |
| 99 | Animal Figure | Leaning Goose | 2.5H | 1948-50 |

There are two mold numbers in the two-digit category: 98 and 99 (Figure 2.2-1). One other two-digit number, 50, is believed by a couple of veteran collectors to exist. This number has been found on an electric clock base (Figure 2.2-2). While there is no consensus that this piece was made by Abingdon, it does have the characteristics of high quality, Abingdon-like glaze, texture, and color. Also, it is known that an employee brought an identical piece home during the artware era.

Figure 2.2-1
Upright and Leaning Goose, #98 and #99, respectively. Offered from 1948-1950.

Figure 2.2-2
Clock base with #50 on bottom believed by some (disputed by others) to be made by Abingdon.

2.3 FOUR-DIGIT MOLD NUMBERS

3801	Sculpture	Head LG	11.5H	1936-38
3802	Sculpture	Head SM	8.5H	1936-38
3901	Sculpture	Nescia	16H	1935-7
3902	Sculpture	Scarf Dancer	13H	1935-7
3903	Sculpture	Kneeling Nude	7H	1935-7
3904	Sculpture	Fruit Girl	10H	1937-8
3905b	Chessman	Bishop	4.5H	1937
3905c	Chessman	Castle	4H	1937
3905k	Chessman	King	5.5H	1937
3905n	Chessman	Knight	5H	1937
3905p	Chessman	Pawn	3.5H	1937
3905q	Chessman	Queen	5H	1937
3906	Sculpture	Shep. & Fawn	11.5H	1937-8
9699	Bowl	Shallow SQ	6.25SQ	1950
9700	Bowl	Shallow Oval	10L	1950
9701	Bowl	Oblong Oval	10L	1950

Figure 2.3-1
3801/Large Head vase, 11.5 inches high with 3802/Small Head vase, 8.5 inches high.

There were eleven mold numbers assigned in the four digit category—eight in the 3000 series and three in the 9000 series. All 3000 series pieces are Frances Moody creations, except 3801 and 3802 (see Figures 2.3-1 and 2). The three 9000 series pieces are found in Figure 2.3-3.

Figure 2.3-2
Reprint from one of the catalogs showing all pieces in the 3900 series. All of these pieces were created by Frances Moody and are considered very valuable.

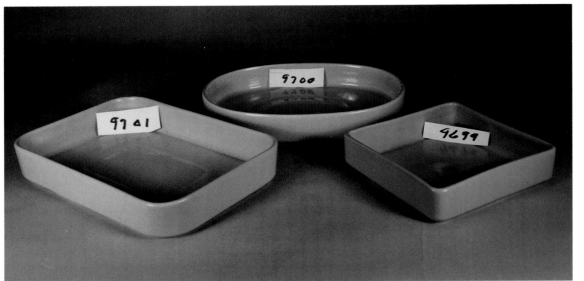

Figure 2.3-3
Three modern bowls—the only pieces in the 9000 series. They were offered after the last catalog was issued in 1950. *Courtesy of Robert Rush.*

2.4 ALPHA-NUMERIC MOLD NUMBERS

(a) A1 through A6, B1 through B6, and C1 through C6 (What Not Vases)

What Not vases came in three sizes: 3.5, 5.0, and 4.5 inches high for the A, B, and C prefixes, respectively. All are rare and sought after by collectors. They were offered in the Fall 1940 and Spring 1941. However, there are inconsistencies in numbering when comparing the two catalogs. Specifically: A6 in the Fall 1940 catalog is different than A6 in the Spring 1941 catalog. The same for B2, B3, and C3. Thus, there are actually twenty-two What Not vases in this series.

Figure 2.4a-1 shows the picture from the Fall 1940 catalog and Figure 2.4a-2 shows the picture from the Spring 1941 catalog. Figures in the remainder of the 2.4a series show modern photos of these vases.

Figure 2.4a-1
Catalog reprint from Fall 1940 showing the What Not vases offered at that time. Compare with those offered in the Spring 1941 catalog.

Figure 2.4a-2
Catalog reprint from Spring 1941. Compare with Spring 1940 catalog shown in previous illustration.

Figure 2.4a-3
What Not vases left to right: A1, A6 (1940 version), A4, 1934 Grand
opening souvenir in blue (back center), A5 (front center), A4, A6
(1940 version). *Courtesy of Robert Rush.*

Figure 2.4a-6
What Not vase B4.

Figure 2.4a-4
More What Not vases back row left to right: C3 (1940 version), B3
(1940 version), C6, C3 (1941 version), B1, C1, C5; front left to
right C2 and A6 (1941 version). *Courtesy of Robert Rush.*

Figure 2.4a-7
What Not vase B2.

Figure 2.4a-5
What Not vases left to right: A6 (1940 version), C5, B6, A4. *Courtesy of Brian and Anita Hickok.*

Figure 2.4a-8
What Not vase B5.

(b) G1 through G4 (Garden and Floor Vases)

G1	Garden Vase	Tall Oil Jar	24x14.5D	1938-50
G2	Garden Vase	Squatty Palm	19.5x18D	1939-50
G3	Floor Vase	Rope	18x12D	1939-50
G4	Floor Vase	Rope SM	14H	1939-50

The G1 and G2 vases (referred to as Garden, Yard, or Solarium vases) are much more rare than the G3 and G4 (Floor Vases). These vases are shown in the 2.4b series of figures.

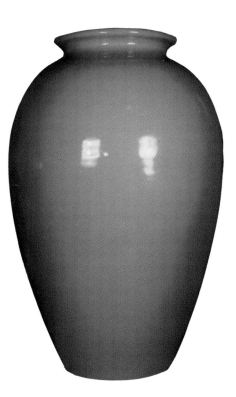

Figure 2.4b-1
G1: Tall Oil Jar (sometimes referred to as Solarium or Garden vase); 24 inches high and 14.5 inches in diameter; offered 1938-1950. *Courtesy of Robert Rush.*

Figure 2.4b-2
G2: Squatty Palm Jar (sometimes referred to as Solarium or Garden vase); 19.5 inches high and 18 inches in diameter; shown here in Royal Blue; offered 1939-1950.

Figure 2.4b-3
G3 and G4: Large and Small Rope vase; G3 is 18 inches high and G4 is 14 inches high. *Courtesy of Robert Rush.*

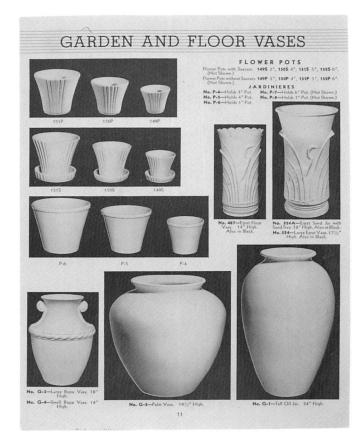

Figure 2.4b-4
Catalog reprint of G1 through G4 and P4 thru P8.

Figure 2-4c shows four of the five jardinieres. These pots were designed to, in turn, hold other less decorative clay pots. The number in the size column represents the height in inches of the clay pot that can fit. inside the jardiniere.

(c) P4 through P8 (Jardinieres)

P4	Jardiniere	*LaFleur*	3	1941-50
P5	Jardiniere	*LaFleur*	4	1941-50
P6	Jardiniere	*LaFleur*	5	1941-50
P7	Jardiniere	*LaFleur*	6	1941-50
P8	Jardiniere	*LaFleur*	7	1941-50

Figure 2.4c-1
P4, 6, 7, and 8: Jardinieres to hold clay pots.

(d) RE1 through RE8 (Refrigerator Ware)

RE1	Refrigerator W	Water Jug	2 Quart	1940
RE2	Refrigerator W	Oblong Leftover		1940
RE3	Refrigerator W	Square Leftover		1940
RE4	Refrigerator W	Butter Dish		1940
RE5	Refrigerator W	Casserole	8L	1940
RE6	Refrigerator W	Round Leftover	6D	1940
RE7	Refrigerator W	Round Leftover	5D	1940
RE8	Refrigerator W	Round Leftover	4D	1940

See Figures 2.4d-1 and 2.

Figure 2.4d-1
RE1-6: Nest of refrigerator ware—all but smallest two round leftover dishes (RE7 and 8). Only offered in 1940. This group came in blue over ivory and in black over yellow.

Figure 2.4d-2
Round leftover dish in black over yellow. This dish came in 4, 5, and 6 inch diameter. *Courtesy of Christine and Jamie Boone.*

Figure 2.4d-3 and 4
Catalog reprint pages of Refrigerator Ware.

2.5 THREE-DIGIT MOLD NUMBERS

(a) Overview

The three-digit mold numbers represent the bulk of the estimated 6,000,000 pieces and 1,000 designs produced from 1934 to 1950. The earliest pieces begin with mold number 301, assigned in 1934; the last mold number assigned was 734 in 1950. However, one 800 series number (861) was assigned to a design called the Egyptian vase, produced before the artware era (such early pieces are referred to in this book as "pre-artware era" pieces). Several different Egyptian style vases were made prior to 1934, as were spittoons, sand jars, and other utility items such as desk pieces and stamp wells.

The three-digit numbers were assigned in rough chronological order with exceptions. Those mold numbers assigned out of chronological sequence were: 1) all numbers in the 100 series; 2) all numbers in the 200 series; 3) a few random numbers in other series. In addition, the following mold numbers have not been found on any pieces of artware nor were they listed in the catalogs: 100; 121-124; 128-129; 134-139; 144-148; 159-169; 182-199; 203-299; 300; 330-333; 617-624; 723; 728; 731; 735.

The 300, 400, and 600 series of numbers took about three to four years each to be assigned. The 500 series was assigned over seven years because of the hiatus caused by WWII and the 700 series was assigned only in 1950, the year artware production was discontinued. Thus, mold numbers in the 300 series were assigned roughly from 1934 to 1937; the 400 series 1937 to 1940; the 500 series 1940 to 1947; the 600 series 1947 to 1950; the 700 series 1950 only. The 100 series was first introduced in 1938 and the 200 series in 1940.

Several of the three-digit mold numbers were modified in the catalogs by an alpha suffix which most often signified a modification to that piece, but on occasion signified a different piece entirely. While the catalogs employed these suffixes to make distinctions, the suffixes were rarely included on the piece itself. The letter "D" was the most often used and stood for "decoration" and indicated that the piece was offered in a hand-painted variety to distinguish it from the single color glaze variety.

Another letter that appeared was the letter "S" which stood for saucer. This letter signified that a flower pot had been modified to include a saucer as part of the design on the bottom of the pot. The letter "P" was later employed intermittently to the unmodified flower pot to distinguish it from the modified pot.

Design 368 (Modern Candleholder) had three suffixes, A, B, and C indicating small, medium and large. This was the only time that the suffixes A, B, and C were used this way. The mold numbers 376F and 376M represented the designs Female Mask and Male Mask, respectively. The mold numbers 378F and 378M represented Small Female Mask and Small Male Mask, respectively. The mold numbers 697DF and 697DP represented cookie jars of identical body design but with the decoration schemes of Floral and Plaid, respectively.

Figure 2.5b-T1
Front page with *Classic* line reprint .

(b) 100 and 200 Series Mold Numbers

The 100 and 200 series are discussed together because both were presented out of chronological sequence and both were atypical groups, being assigned to only a very few different types of pottery. Nearly all pieces in the 100 series belong to two lines of floral ware that were first introduced in 1938: the *Classic* line which was mostly vases and the *LaFleur* line which was mostly flower pots. *Classic* vases came in 13 shapes. In addition, many of these shapes came in one or more of six possible sizes (10, 9, 8, 7, 6, and 5.5 inches high). The 13 different shapes are shown in Figures 2.5b-1 through 13. Two console bowls and a set of candlesticks were given the numbers 125 through 127 (Figures 2.5b-14 and 15) and 113 was assigned to a refrigerator water jug (Figure 2.5b-16). In 1950, six other vases called Floral vases with no indication that they were to be considered part of the *Classic* line were introduced with the mold numbers 176 through 181 (Figures 2.5b-17 through 19).

Figure 2.5b-1 ALPHA shape. Made in five sizes (mold numbers and height in inches/years made): 101/10H/1938-49; 150/9H/1941-42; 105/8H/1938-40; 109/6H/1938-41. Not shown: 170/7H/1941. *Courtesy of Robert Rush*.

Figure 2.5b-2 BETA shape. Made in the three sizes: 102/10H/1938-39; 106/8H/1938-40; and 110/6H/1938-41. *Courtesy of Robert Rush*.

Figure 2.5b-3 GAMMA shape. Made in three sizes: 103/10H/1938-39; 107/8H/1938-39; 111/6H/1938-39. *Courtesy of Robert Rush*.

Figure 2.5b-4
DELTA shape.
Made in three
sizes: 104/10H/
1938; 108/8H/
1938-39; and
112/6H/1938-39.

Figure 2.5b-5
Made in four
sizes: 114/10H/
1939-46; 132/8H/
1940; 142/5.5H/
1940-41; and
171/7H/1941.
*Courtesy of
Christine and
Jamie Boone.*

Figure 2.5b-6
Made in five sizes:
115/10H/1939-
49; 133/8H/1940;
and 143/5.5H/
1940-41. Not
shown: 151/9H/
41-42 and 172/
7H/1941.
*Courtesy of Robert
Rush.*

Figure 2.5b-7
Made in two sizes: 152/9H/1941-42. Not shown: 116/10H/1939-49.

Figure 2.5b-8
Made in five sizes: 117/10H/1939-49; 130/8H/1940; 140/5.5H/1940-41. Not shown: 153/9H/1941-42; 173/7H/1941.

Figure 2.5b-9
Made in three sizes: 118/10H/1940-42; 131/8H/1940; 141/5.5H/1940-41.

Figure 2.5b-10
Made in two sizes: 119/10H/1947-49; 154/9H/1941-42.

Figure 2.5b-11
Made in two sizes: 120/10H/1947-49;
155/9H/1941-42. *Courtesy of Christine
and Jamie Boone.*

Figure 2.5b-12
Made in only one size: 174/7H/1941.

Figure 2.5b-13
Made in two sizes:
156/9H/1941-42.
Not shown: 175/
7H/1941.

Figure 2.5b-14
Large *Classic*
console bowl 127/
14 inches x 6.5H/
1940-41 with
candlesticks 126/2
inches x 3.5H/
1940-41.

Figure 2.5b-15
Small *Classic*
console bowl 125/
11 x 6.25H/1940-
41 with candle-
sticks 126/2 x
3.5H/1940-41.

Figure 2.5b-16
Refrigerator Water Jug 113/7.5H/1938. *Courtesy of Elaine Westover.*

Figure 2.5b-17
Floral vase 176/10H/1950.

Figure 2.5b-18
Floral vase 177/10H/1950. *Courtesy of Brian and Anita Hickok.*

Figure 2.5b-19
Four Floral vases 178-181/10H/1950.

The remaining pieces assigned 100 series mold numbers were part of the *LaFleur* line of floral ware. This line consisted mainly of flower pots. Pots were first produced in solid colors, then solid colors with saucers attached to the bottom, and finally, in hand-painted varieties. Also, candleholders in this shape were issued as were saucers or bowls for holding pots and other garden items. See the catalog reprint in Figure 2.5b-20 and photos in Figures 2.5b-20b through 22.

The numbers 149 through 158 were on two different shapes. For example, 150 is stamped on a *Classic* vase as shown in Figure 2.5b-1 AND on a *LaFleur* flower pot like the type shown in Figure 2.5b-20 through 22.

There are seven known mold numbers assigned in the 200 series: three for pitchers (200 through 202 which were advertised with the *Classic* line and had *Classic* labels) and four for lamp bases (253, 254, 256, and 258). Figure 2.5b-23 shows the three pitchers while Figures 2.5b-24 through 26 show three of the four lamp bases.

Figure 2.5b-20a
Catalog reprint of *LaFleur* gardenware. The three inch pot with the mold number 149 was later added.

Figure 2.5b-20b
Advertised in catalogs as being in four sizes (149-152/3, 4, 5, and 6 inches high respectively). However, there appears to be one size missing in this Photo which would make five sizes. The smallest piece should be the candlestick 158. The pieces shown here are the earliest *LaFleur* pots in solid colors. Pots were later modified to include a saucer and still later were hand-painted as shown in the next two illustrations.

Figure 2.5b-21
Nest of four *LaFleur* pots (149S-152S/3, 4, 5, and 6 inches high) with saucers attached during production.

Figure 2.5b-22
Nest of four *LaFleur* pots (149D-152D/3, 4, 5, and 6 inches high) with hand-painted decorations.

Figure 2.5b-23
Three pitchers in the 200 mold number series (200/2quart/1940-41 and 202/1 pint/1940-41; 201/1 quart/1940-41). *Courtesy of Christine and Jamie Boone.*

Figure 2.5b-24
Swirl Shaft lamp base (252). *Courtesy of Robert Rush.*

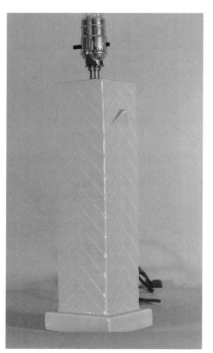

Figure 2.5b-25
Drape Shaft lamp base (254). *Courtesy of Robert Rush.*

Figure 2.5b-26
Square Shaft lamp base (256). *Courtesy of Robert Rush.*

(c) 300 through 700 Mold Numbers

Most Abingdon Pottery artware was assigned a mold number in the 300 to 700 series of numbers and most of these numbers were assigned in chronological order, with only a few exceptions being out of chronological sequence. The following Artware Gallery provides pictures of all pieces in the 300 through 700 series of numbers with a caption that provides the mold number, the dimensions and the years of production. Pre-artware era pieces and pieces with no mold number assigned are also shown after the 700 series numbers.

Figure 2.5c-3
303/Cornucopia/7.5H/1934-36.

Figure 2.5c-1
301/Jar/Ming/7.25H/1934-36.

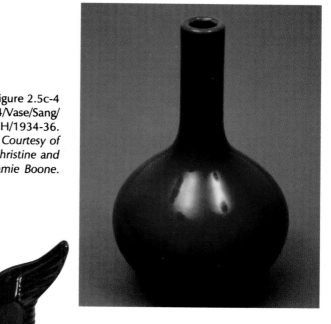

Figure 2.5c-4
304/Vase/Sang/
9.5H/1934-36.
*Courtesy of
Christine and
Jamie Boone.*

Figure 2.5c-2
302/Vase/Lung/11
H/1934-38.
*Courtesy of Robert
Rush.*

Figure 2.5c-5
305/Bookend/Seagull/6H/1934-46.
Courtesy of Christine and Jamie Boone.

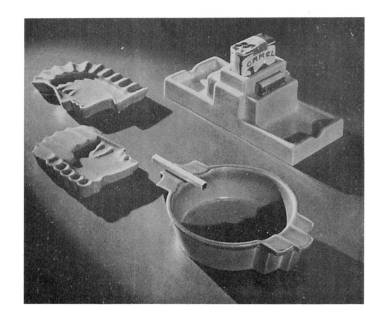

Figure 2.5c-6
306/Ashtray/Abingdon/8 x 3/1934-36 with 316/Ashtray/Trojan/5 x 3.5/1934-36; 317/Ashtray/Round/5D/1934-37; and 326/Ashtray/Greek/4.25 x 3/1934-36.

Figure 2.5c-7
307/Vase/Fairfield/11H/1934-37.

Figure 2.5c-8
308/Jar/Coolie/11H/1934-38, 1947.

Figure 2.5c-9
309/Vase/Neo-Classic/12.5H/1934-36. *Courtesy of Robert Rush.*

Figure 2.5c-10
310/Jar/Chang/10.5H/1934-36.

Figure 2.5c-11
311/Bowl/Flower/6.5D/1934-36. *Courtesy of Robert Rush.*

Figure 2.5c-12
312/Vase/Han/6H/1934-49. *Courtesy of Christine and Jamie Boone.*

Figure 2.5c-13
313/Bowl/Rope Salad Bowl/10.5D/1934-36 with 323/Candleholder/Rope/3.75D/1934-36 and 324/Vase/Rope/6H/1934-38, 1947-48.

Figure 2.5c-14
314/Vase/Swedish/8.25H/1934-36. *Courtesy of Christine and Jamie Boone.*

Figure 2.5c-15
315/Vase/
Athenian/9H/
1934-36, 1947.

Figure 2.5c-18
318/Vase/Ring/
10.25H/1934-37.
*Courtesy of Robert
Rush.*

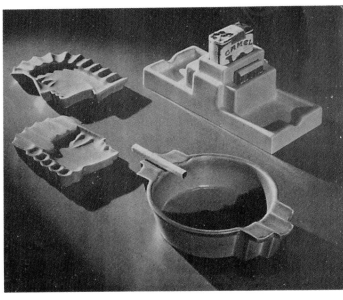

Figure 2.5c-19
319/Vase/Modern
#1/7.25H/1934-
36. *Courtesy of
Brian and Anita
Hickok.*

Figure 2.5c-16
316/Ashtray/Trojan/5 x 3.5/1934-36 with 306/Ashtray/Abingdon/
8 x 3/1934-36; 317/Ashtray/Round/5D/1934-37; and 326/Ash-
tray/Greek/4.25 x 3/1934-36.

Figure 2.5c-17
317/Ashtray/
Round/5D/1934-
37 Dubonnet at
center of Photo
with 334 in
Gunmetal Black
and brown, 555 in
Black, and 551 in
green. *Courtesy of
Robert Rush.*

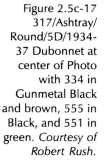

Figure 2.5c-20
320/Vase/Tulip/4H/1936-1937. *Courtesy of Robert Rush.*

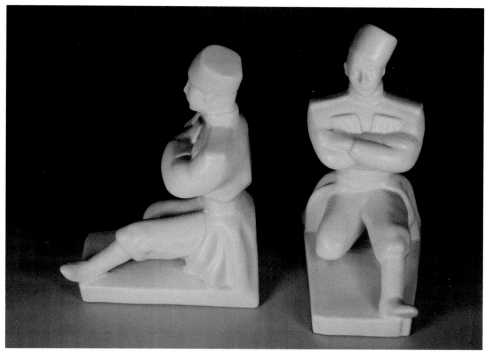

Figure 2.5c-21
321/Bookend/Russian/6.5H/1934-40.
Courtesy of Robert Rush.

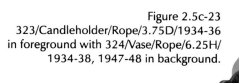

Figure 2.5c-22
322/Goblet/Swedish/6.5H/1934-36, 1947.

Figure 2.5c-24
325 /Vase/Chien/
6.5H/1934-37, 1947.

Figure 2.5c-23
323/Candleholder/Rope/3.75D/1934-36
in foreground with 324/Vase/Rope/6.25H/
1934-38, 1947-48 in background.

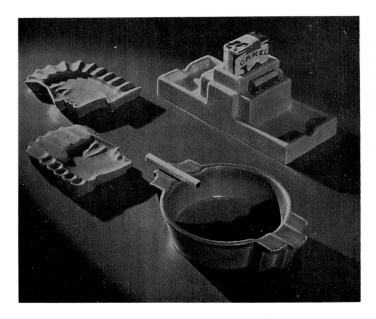

Figure 2.5c-25
326/Ashtray/Greek/4.25 x 3/1934-36 with 316/Ashtray/Trojan/5 x 3.5/1934-36 with 306/Ashtray/Abingdon/8 x 3/1934-36; and 317/Ashtray/Round/5D/1934-37.

Figure 2.5c-26
327/Vase/Modern #2/6H/1934-36. *Courtesy of Christine and Jamie Boone.*

Figure 2.5c-27
328/Vase/Modern #3/4.5H/1934-36. *Courtesy of Knoxville Museum.*

Figure 2.5c-28
329/Stand for vase/3.5D/1935-37. *Courtesy of Christine and Jamie Boone.*
Note: mold numbers 330-333 were never assigned.

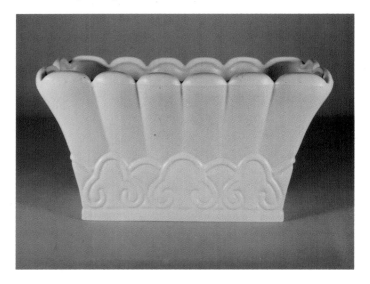

Figure 2.5c-29
334/Ashtray/Utility/5.5D/1935-37.

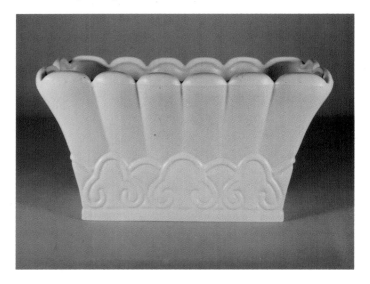

Figure 2.5c-30
335/Vase/Chinese Scalloped Rectangle/10.5L/1935-38.

Figure 2.5c-31
336/Bowl/Square/9SQ/1935-41 with
336A/Candleholder/Hurricane (with
glass)/11H/1939-41.

Figure 2.5c-32
337/Desert Dish/Square/5SQ/1935. *Courtesy of Christine and Jamie Boone.*

Figure 2.5c-33
338/Bowl/Square Covered/4.75SQ/1935.

Figure 2.5c-34
339/Plate/Square
Salad/7.5SQ/1935
in brown on pink
340/Plate/Square
Service/10.5 SQ/
1935. Also in
picture: 341/Bowl/
Coupe Soup/
5.5D/1935 in Fire
Red; 342/Plate/
Coupe Salad/
7.5D/1935 in
brown on black
343/Plate/Coupe
Service/12D/
1935; green 337/
Desert Dish/
Square/5SQ/1935
in rear of plates.
*Courtesy of Robert
Rush.*

Figure 2.5c-35
344/Plate/Wild Rose/10 x 12/1935-36. *Courtesy of Brian and Anita Hickok.*

Figure 2.5c-37
346/Flower Pot/Ring Stand/5.5D/1935-36 with 347/Flower Pot/ Egg & Dart/7.25D/1935-37.

Figure 2.5c-36
345/Bowl/Chinese Oval/9 x 11/1935-37. *Courtesy of Robert Rush.*

Figure 2.5c-38
347/Flower Pot/Egg & Dart/7.25D/1935-37. *Courtesy of Robert Rush.*

Figure 2.5c-39
348/Box (Cigarette)/Trix/4.75 x 3.75/1935-37, 1947. *Courtesy of Robert Rush.*

Figure 2.5c-40
349/Chalice/5.5H/1935-37 with 355/Candleholder/Eiffel/4.75H/1935-36; 361/Bowl/Triform/8 x 14.5/1935-37; and 362/Bowl/Monoform/6D/1935-36.

Figure 2.5c-41
350/Vase/Fleur/7H/1935-38, 1947. *Courtesy of Brian and Anita Hickok.*

Figure 2.5c-42
351/Vase/Capri/5.75H/1935-37. *Courtesy of Robert Rush.*

Figure 2.5c-44
353/Vase/Penthouse/1935-38.

Figure 2.5c-43
352/Vase/Echo/4H/1935-40 with 312/Vase/Han/6H/1934-49.
Courtesy of Christine and Jamie Boone.

Figure 2.5c-45
354/Box/Trixtra/2 x 3/1935-37 with 317/Ashtray/Round/5D/1934-37; 334/Ashtray/Utility/5.5D/1935-37; 348/Box (Cigarette)/Trix/4.74 x 3.75/1935-37, 1947; 371/Ashtray/Petite/4D/1936-37; 386/Ashtray/Daisy/4.5D/1936-37.

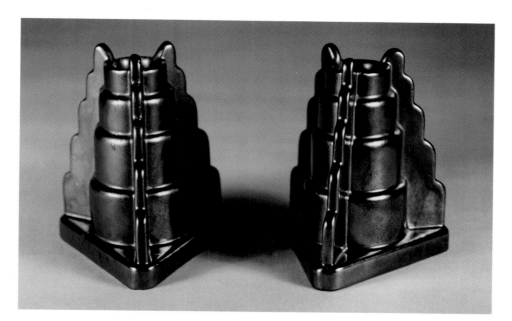

Figure 2.5c-46
355/Candleholder/Eiffel/4.75H/1935-36.

Figure 2.5c-47
356/Ashtray/Duo/6.75 x 3.5/1936 with
334/Ashtray/Utility/5.5D/1935-37; 348/
Box (Cigarette)/Trix/4.74 x 3.75/1935-37,
1947; 354/Box/Trixtra/2 x 3/1935-37.

Figure 2.5c-48
357/Vase/Salon/14H/1935-38. *Courtesy
of Knoxville Museum.*

Figure 2.5c-49
358/Flower Pot/Ionic/5H/1935-37 with
359/Flower Pot/Mart/3.5H/1935-37.

Figure 2.5c-50
358a/Flower Pot/Ionic LG/10.5D/1937 shown at lower center with (in clockwise order beginning at immediate left of 358a) 335/Vase/ Chinese Scalloped Rectangle/10.5L/1935-38; 318/Vase/Ring/ 10.25H/1934-37; 307/Vase/Fairfield/11H/1934-37; 373/Vase/ Manhattan/12.5H/1936-37; 302/Lung vase/11H/1934-38; and 415/Plate/Apple Blossom/11.5D/1937.

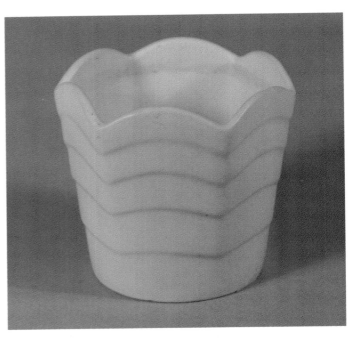

Figure 2.5c-51
359/Flower Pot/Mart/3.5H/1935-37. *Courtesy of Robert Rush.*

Figure 2.5c-52
360/Candleholder/Quatrain/3SQ/1935-36. *Courtesy of Robert Rush.*

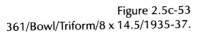

Figure 2.5c-53
361/Bowl/Triform/8 x 14.5/1935-37.

Figure 2.5c-54
362/Bowl/Monoform/6D/1935-36 with 361/Bowl/Triform/8 x 14.5/1935-37; 355/Candleholder/Eiffel/4.75H/1935-36; and 349/Chalice/5.5H/1935-37.

Figure 2.5c-55
363/Bookend/Colt/6H/1935-38.

Figure 2.5c-56
364/Jar/Elite/4.5H/1936.

Figure 2.5c-57
365/Jar/Dart Candy/6.25D/1936-37. *Courtesy of Christine and Jamie Boone.*

Figure 2.5c-58
366/Flower Pot/Egg & Dart MD/5.25H/1936-37. *Courtesy of Christine and Jamie Boone.*

Figure 2.5c-59
367/Flower Pot/Egg & Dart SM/4.5H/1936-37. *Courtesy of Christine and Jamie Boone.*

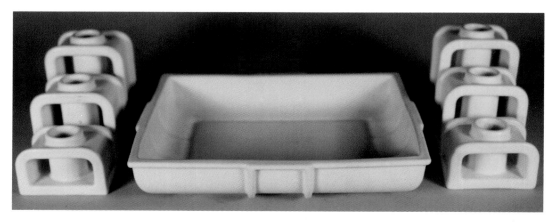

Figure 2.5c-60
368a/Candleholder/Modern SM/2H/1936-38; 368b/Candleholder/Modern MD/3H/1936-38; 368c/Candleholder/Modern LG/4H/1936-38; 394/Bowl/Modern Blossom Boat/8 x 10/1936-38. *Courtesy of Robert Rush.*

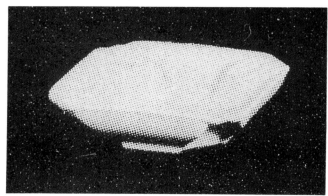

Figure 2.5c-61
369/Ashtray/Guard/5SQ/1936.

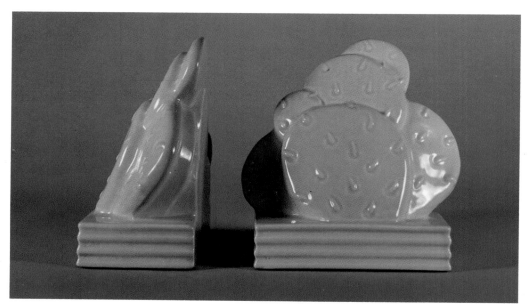

Figure 2.5c-62
370/Bookend/Cactus/6H/1936-38. *Courtesy of Knoxville Museum.*

Figure 2.5c-63
371/Ashtray/Petite/4D/1936-37 with 354/Box/Trixtra/2 x 3/1935-37; 317/Ashtray/Round/5D/1934-37; 334/Ashtray/Utility/5.5D/1935-37; 348/Box (Cigarette)/Trix/4.74 x 3.75/1935-37, 1947; 386/Ashtray/Daisy/4.5D/1936-37.

Figure 2.5c-64
372/Vase/Rhythm/10H/1936-37 with 381/
Vase/Rhythm SM/5.5H/1936-37. Same
design as 380/Vase/Rhythm MD/7.
Courtesy of Robert Rush.

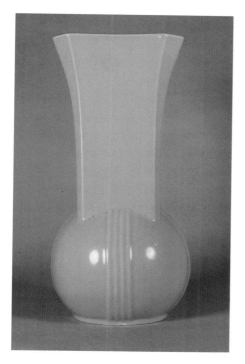

Figure 2.5c-65
373/Vase/Manhattan/12.5H/1936-37.
Courtesy of Robert Rush.

Figure 2.5c-66
374/Bookend/Cactus Planter/7H/1936-38.
Courtesy of Robert Rush.

Figure 2.5c-67
375/Wall Pocket/M Glory Double/6.5H/1936-40.

Figure 2.5c-68
376F/Wall Mask/
Female LG/7.5H/
1936. Same
design as 378F/
Wall Mask/Female
SM/4H/1936.
*Courtesy of
Christine and
Jamie Boone.*

Figure 2.5c-69
376M/Wall Mask/
Male LG/7.5H/
1936. Same
design as 378M/
Wall Mask/Male
SM/4.0H/1936.
*Courtesy of Robert
Rush.*

Figure 2.5c-70
377/Wall Pocket/
M Glory/7.5H/
1936-50.

Figure 2.5c-71
379/Wall Pocket/
Daisy/7.75D/
1936-41.

Figure 2.5c-72
380/Vase/Rhythm
MD/7.75H/1936-
37. Same design
as 381/Vase/
Rhythm SM/5.5H/
1936-37 and 372/
Vase/Rhythm/10H/
1936-37. *Courtesy
of Christine and
Jamie Boone.*

Figure 2.5c-73
382/Bowl/Daisy LG/12.25D/1936-38;
383/Bowl/Daisy SM/9.5D/1936-38; 384/
Candleholder/Daisy/4.5D/1936-38; NOT
SHOWN: 385/Bowl/Daisy Nut Dish/3.5D/
1936; NOT SHOWN: 386/Ashtray/Daisy/
4.5D/1936-37; 387/Plate /Daisy Salad/
7.5D/1936-37. *Courtesy of Robert Rush.*

Figure 2.5c-74
388/Animal Figure/Pouter Pigeon/4.25H/
1936-37, 1942-46.

Figure 2.5c-75
389/Vase/Geranium/7H/1936-37.
Courtesy of Robert Rush.

Figure 2.5c-77
393/Bowl/M
Glory/7D/1936-
38. *Courtesy of
Brian and Anita
Hickok.*

Figure 2.5c-76
390/Vase/M Glory LG/10H/1936-39.
Same design as 391/Vase/M Glory MD/
7.75H/1936-38 and 392/Vase/M Glory
SM/5.5H/1936-38. *Courtesy of Brian and
Anita Hickok.*

Figure 2.5c-78
394/Bowl/Modern Blossom Boat/8 x 10/1936-38 with 368A/Candleholder/Modern SM/2H/1936-38; 368B/Candleholder/Modern MD/3H/1936-38; 368C/Candleholder/Modern LG/4H/1936-38. *Courtesy of Robert Rush.*

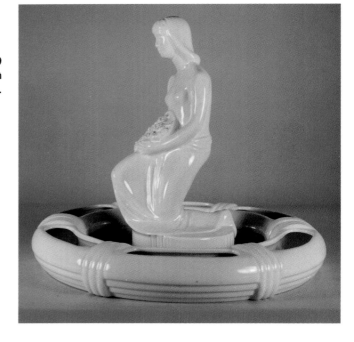

Figure 2.5c-79
395/Arc-De-Fleur/11.5D/1936-38 with Fruit Girl 3904/10H/1937-38.

Figure 2.5c-80
396/Flower Pot/LG/7SQ/1936-38. Same design as 397/Flower Pot/MD/5.75SQ/1936-38 and 398/Flower Pot/SM/4.5SQ/1936-38. *Courtesy of Christine and Jamie Boone.*

Figure 2.5c-81
399/Bowl/Daisy SM/6.5D/1937-38. *Courtesy of Christine and Jamie Boone.*

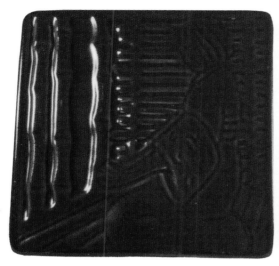

Figure 2.5c-82
400/Teapot Tile/
Geisha/5SQ/1937-
38 and 401/
Teapot Tile/
Coolie/5SQ/1937-
38.

Figure 2.5c-83
402/Vase/Box/5.5H/1937-38. *Courtesy of
Brian and Anita Hickok.*

Figure 2.5c-84
403/Bowl/Chain/8.5 x 12.5/1937-38 with
404/Candleholder/Triple Chain/3 x 8.5/
1937-38; 406/Candleholder/Leaf/3D/
1937; 408/Bowl/Leaf/6.5D/1937.

Figure 2.5c-85
404/Candleholder/Triple Chain/3 x 8.5/
1937-38. *Courtesy of Robert Rush.*

Figure 2.5c-86
405/Vase/
Crosspatch/8H/
1937-38. *Courtesy
of Brian and Anita
Hickok.*

Figure 2.5c-87
407/Bowl/Rose/6D/1937-38.

Figure 2.5c-88
408/Bowl/Leaf/6.5D/1937.

Figure 2.5c-89
409/Bowl/Volute/6D/1937-39; 410/Vase/
Volute SM/8H/1937-39; 411/Vase/Volute
MD/10.5H/1937-40; 412/Vase Floor/
Volute LG/15H/1937-40. *Courtesy of
Robert Rush.*

Figure 2.5c-90
413/Bowl/Wreath/12D/1937.

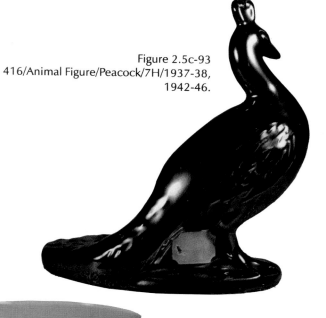

Figure 2.5c-93
416/Animal Figure/Peacock/7H/1937-38,
1942-46.

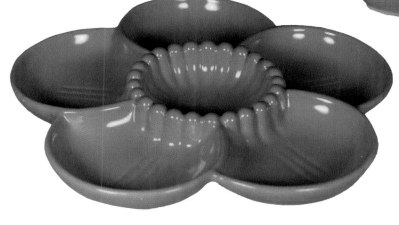

Figure 2.5c-91
414/Candleholder/Wreath/4D/1937.

Figure 2.5c-94
417/Vase/Scroll/
8H/1937-38.

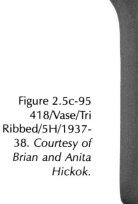

Figure 2.5c-92
415/Plate/Apple Blossom/11.5D/1937. *Courtesy of Robert Rush.*

Figure 2.5c-95
418/Vase/Tri
Ribbed/5H/1937-
38. *Courtesy of
Brian and Anita
Hickok.*

Figure 2.5c-96
419/Bowl/Rhythm/5D/1937 at bottom second from left with 320/Vase/Tulip/4H/1936-1937 on immediate left; 400/Teapot Tile/Geisha/5SQ/1937-38 and 401/Teapot Tile/Coolie/5SQ/1937-38 on immediate right; 349/Chalice/5.5H/1935-37 at top; 418/Vase/Tri Ribbed/5H/1937-38 at center left; 359/Flower Pot/Mart/3.5H/1935-37 at middle center; and 352/Vase/Echo/4H/1935-40.

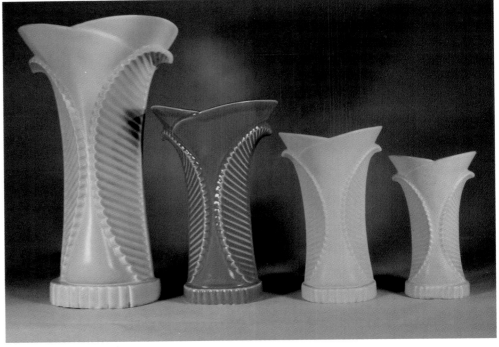

Figure 2.5c-97
420/Vase/Fern Leaf/7.25H/1937-38; 421/Vase/Fern Leaf/8.75H/1937-38; 422/Vase/Fern Leaf/10.25H/1937-39; 433/Vase Floor/Fern Leaf/15H/1937-39. *Courtesy of Robert Rush.*

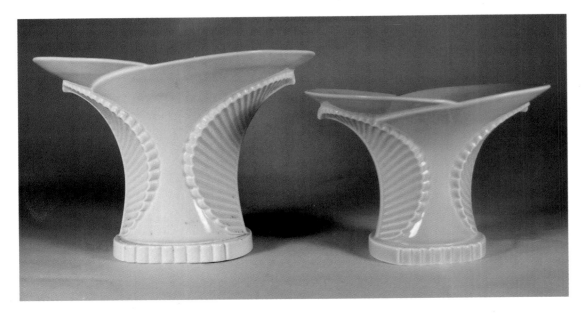

Figure 2.5c-98
423/Bowl/Fern Leaf/7.25H/1937-38; 424/Bowl/Fern Leaf/8.5H/1937-38; not shown: 425/Bowl/Fern Leaf/10.5H/1937-38. *Courtesy of Robert Rush.*

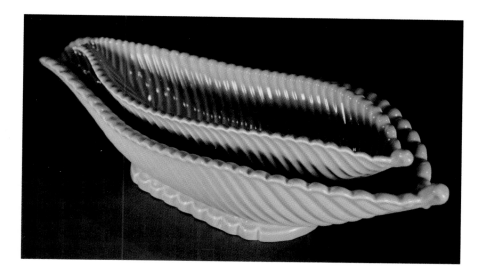

Figure 2.5c-99
426/Flower Boat/Fern Leaf/13 x 4/1937-38 (inside) and 432/Fruit
Boat/Fern Leaf/15 x 6.5/1938-39 (outside).

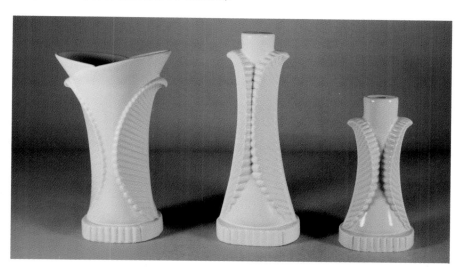

Figure 2.5c-100
427/Candleholder/Fern Leaf/5.5H/1937-38; 429/Candleholder/
Fern Leaf/8H/1937-38; 420/Vase/Fern Leaf/7.25H/1937-38.

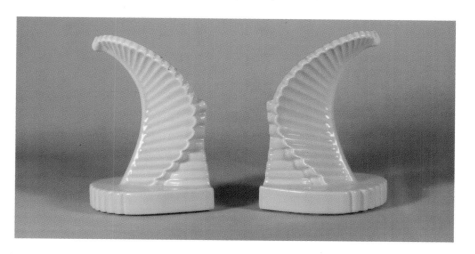

Figure 2.5c-101
428/Bookend/Fern Leaf/5.5H/1937-38. *Courtesy of Robert Rush.*

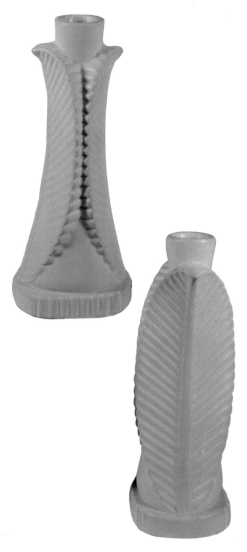

Figure 2.5c-102
429/Candleholder/Fern Leaf/8H/1937-38.
Courtesy of Knoxville Museum.

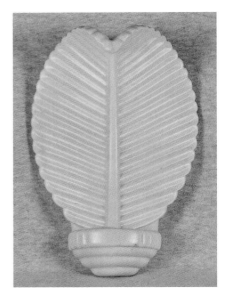

Figure 2.5c-103
430/Pitcher/Fern
Leaf/8H/1937-38.

Figure 2.5c-104
431/Wall Pocket/
Fern Leaf/7.5H/
1937-38.

Figure 2.5c-105
432/Fruit Boat/
Fern Leaf/15 x
6.5/1938-39 with
426/Flower Boat/
Fern Leaf/13 x 4/
1937-38. *Courtesy
of Robert Rush.*

Figure 2.5c-106
433/Vase Floor/Fern Leaf/15H/1937-39.

Figure 2.5c-107
434/
Candleholder/Fern
Leaf Boat/3 x 5.5/
1938 with 426/
Flower Boat/Fern
Leaf/13 x 4/1937-
38.

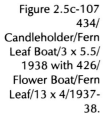

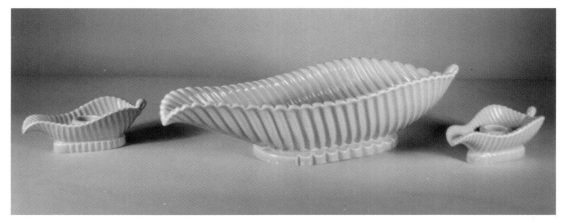

Figure 2.5c-108
435/Wall Pocket/Fern Leaf Tri/8W/1938-40.

Figure 2.5c-111
438/Vase/Han Square/6SQ/1938-41. *Courtesy of Christine and Jamie Boone.*

Figure 2.5c-109
436/Candleholder/Fern Leaf Tri /3 x 8/ 1938-39 with 434/ Candleholder/Fern Leaf Boat/3 x 5.5/ 1938 and 427/ Candleholder/Fern Leaf/5.5H/1937-38. *Courtesy of Robert Rush.*

Figure 2.5c-110
437/Bowl/Han Pansy/4 x 10.5/1938-50.

Figure 2.5c-112
439/Candleholder/Han Single/3SQ/1938. *Courtesy of Christine and Jamie Boone.*

Figure 2.5c-113
440/Candleholder/Han Triple/3 x 7.5/1938 with 336/Bowl/Square/9SQ/1935-41.

Figure 2.5c-114
441/Bookend/Horsehead/7H/1938-50.

Figure 2.5c-116
444/Bookend/Vase/Dolphin/5.75H/1938-49.

Figure 2.5c-115
442/Vase/Laurel SM/5.5H/1938-39 with 443/Vase/Laurel LG/8H/1938-39. *Courtesy of Robert Rush.*

Figure 2.5c-117
445/Vase/Laced Cuff SM/8H/1938-39
with 446/Vase/Laced Cuff LG/10H/1938-39. *Courtesy of Robert Rush.*

Figure 2.5c-118
447/Candleholder/Sunburst/8L/1938.

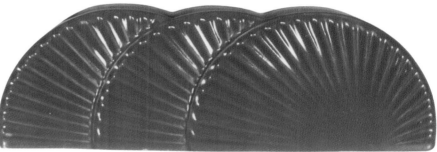

Figure 2.5c-119
448/Window Box/Sunburst/9L/1938-39.

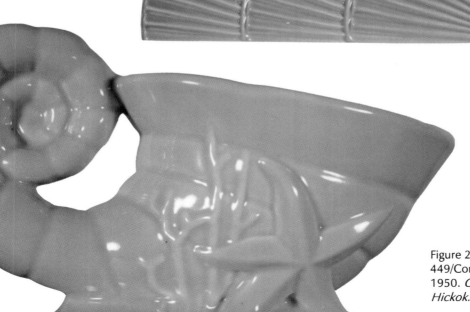

Figure 2.5c-120
449/Cornucopia/Shell/4.5H/1938-39,
1950. *Courtesy of Brian and Anita Hickok.*

Figure 2.5c-121
450/Bowl/Asters
Flare/11.5 x 7.5/
1938-40 with 451/
Candleholder/
Asters Double/
4.5H/1938-40.
Courtesy of Robert Rush.

Figure 2.5c-122
452/Bowl/Asters LG/15 x 9/1938-40.

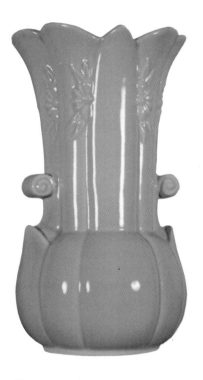

Figure 2.5c-124
454/Bowl/Asters
Round/6.5D/
1938-40.

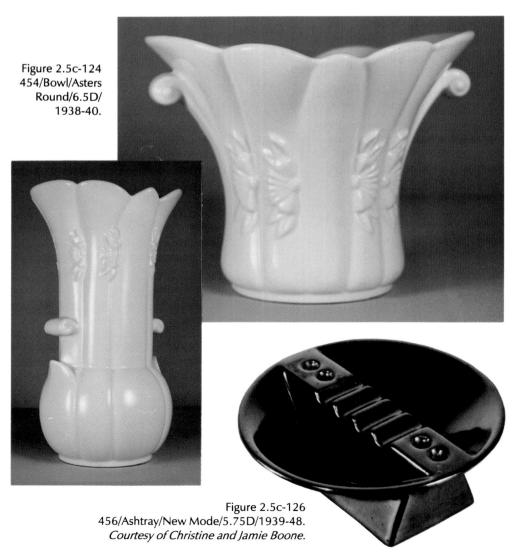

Figure 2.5c-123
453/Vase/Asters SM/8H/1938-39.
Courtesy of Brian and Anita Hickok.

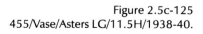

Figure 2.5c-125
455/Vase/Asters LG/11.5H/1938-40.

Figure 2.5c-126
456/Ashtray/New Mode/5.75D/1939-48.
Courtesy of Christine and Jamie Boone.

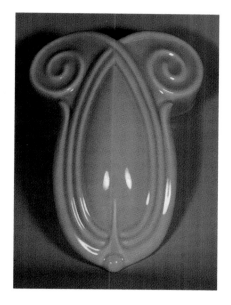

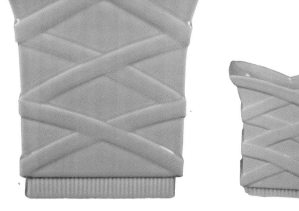

Figure 2.5c-127
457/Wall Pocket/
Ionic/9H/1939.
*Courtesy of Robert
Rush.*

Figure 2.5c-128
458/Vase/Lattice/
5.5H/1939 with
459/Vase/Lattice/
10.25H/1939-41.
*Courtesy of Robert
Rush.*

Figure 2.5c-129
460/Bowl/Panel/8D/1939 with 461/Candleholder/Panel/2.5H/
1939. *Courtesy of Robert Rush.*

Figure 2.5c-131
463/Vase/Star/
7.5H/1939-50.

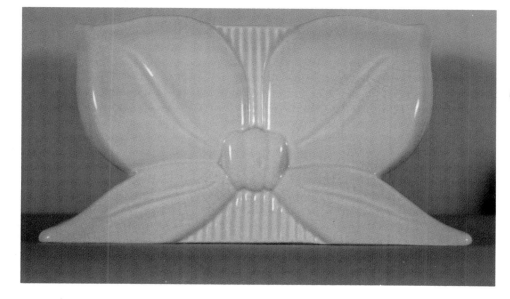

Figure 2.5c-130
462/Vase/Ribbon/4.5H/1939-50. *Courtesy of Brian and Anita Hickok.*

Figure 2.5c-132
464/Vase/Medallion/8H/1939-40.

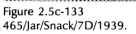

Figure 2.5c-133
465/Jar/Snack/7D/1939.

Figure 2.5c-136
468/Vase/Bird/7.5H/1939-40. *Courtesy of Brian and Anita Hickok.*

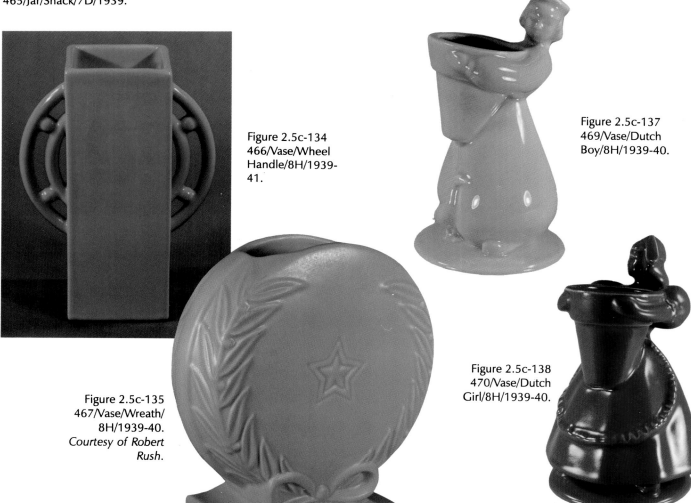

Figure 2.5c-134
466/Vase/Wheel
Handle/8H/1939-
41.

Figure 2.5c-137
469/Vase/Dutch
Boy/8H/1939-40.

Figure 2.5c-135
467/Vase/Wreath/
8H/1939-40.
*Courtesy of Robert
Rush.*

Figure 2.5c-138
470/Vase/Dutch
Girl/8H/1939-40.

Figure 2.5c-139
471/Cookie Jar/Little Ol' lady/7.25D/1939-46. *Courtesy of Brian and Anita Hickok.*

Figure 2.5c-140
472/Vase/Reed/8H/1939.

Figure 2.5c-141
473/Bowl/Combination/12 x 7/1939 with 469/Vase/Dutch Boy/8H/1939-40 and 470/Vase/Dutch Girl/8H/1939-40. *Courtesy of Robert Rush.*

Figure 2.5c-142
474/Cornucopia/Single/5H/1939-50. *Courtesy of Brian and Anita Hickok.*

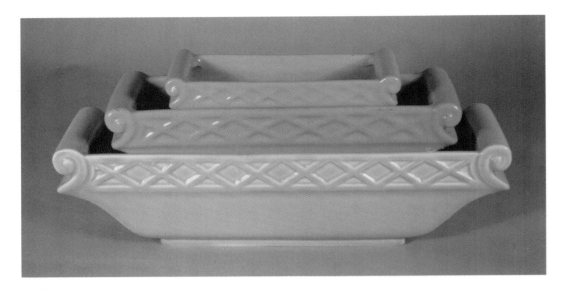

Figure 2.5c-143 475/Window Box SM/7L/1939-40 with 476/Window Box MD/10.5L/1939-50 and 477/Window Box LG/13.5L/1939-41. *Courtesy of Robert Rush.*

Figure 2.5c-144 478/Bowl/Scroll SM/11.5L/1939-41. *Courtesy of Christine and Jamie Boone.*

Figure 2.5c-145 479/Candleholder/Scroll Double/4.5H/1939-50 with 480/Bowl/Scroll LG/17.5L/1939-50.

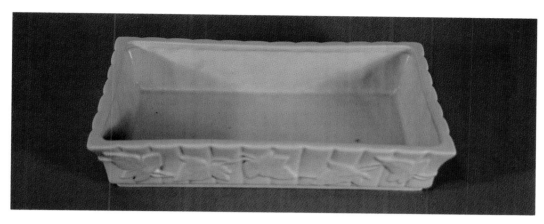

Figure 2.5c-146
481/Bowl/Ivy/12 x
7/1939-41.
*Courtesy of
Christine and
Jamie Boone.*

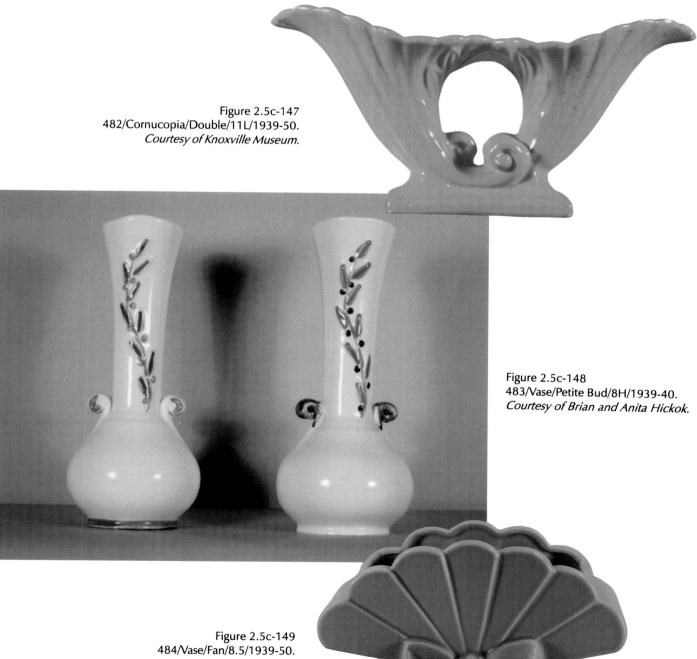

Figure 2.5c-147
482/Cornucopia/Double/11L/1939-50.
Courtesy of Knoxville Museum.

Figure 2.5c-148
483/Vase/Petite Bud/8H/1939-40.
Courtesy of Brian and Anita Hickok.

Figure 2.5c-149
484/Vase/Fan/8.5/1939-50.

Figure 2.5c-150
485/Vase/Acanthus SM/8H/1939-40 with 486/Vase/Acanthus LG/
11H/1939-50.

Figure 2.5c-152
488/Ashtray/Box/4 x 3.25/1939-40.
Courtesy of Christine and Jamie Boone.

Figure 2.5c-153
489/Wall Pocket/
Dutch Boy/10H/
1939.

Figure 2.5c-154
490/Wall Pocket/
Dutch Girl/10H/
1939.

Figure 2.5c-151
487/vase Floor/Egret SM/14H/1939-50 with 524/Vase/Floor/Egret
LG/17.5H/1940-50. *Courtesy of Brian and Anita Hickok.*

Figure 2.5c-155
491/Vase/Flower Holding/5H/1940-50.

Figure 2.5c-156
492/Vase/Small Bowl/4H/1940. *Courtesy of Betty Perry. Photo taken by Tom Foley of Midwest Photo.*

Figure 2.5c-157
493/Wall Pocket/Double/8.5H/1940.
Courtesy of Robert Rush.

Figure 2.5c-159
495/Cookie Jar/Fat Boy/8.25 x 6/1940-46.
Courtesy of Elaine Westover.

Figure 2.5c-160
496D/Vase/Hollyhock/7H/1947-48.

Figure 2.5c-158
494/Vase/Ship/7.5H/1940-46.

Figure 2.5c-161
497D/Vase/
Blackamoor/7.5H/
1940.

Figure 2.5c-162
498/Window Box/
Han LG/14.5L/
1940-41.

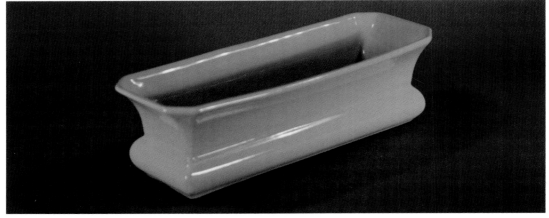

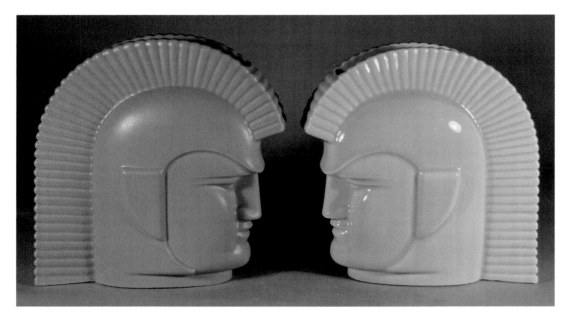

Figure 2.5c-163
499/Bookend/
Vase/Trojan Head/
7.5H/1940-41.

Figure 2.5c-164
500/Bowl/Shell LG/15L/1940-49/ with 501/Bowl/Shell MD/10.5L/
1940-48; 502/Bowl/Shell SM/7L/1940-4; and 533/Bowl/Shell/12L/
1941-50. *Courtesy of Christine and Jamie Boone.*

Figure 2.5c-167
505/Candleholder/Shell Double/4H/1940-
49.

Figure 2.5c-165
503/Candleholder/Shell Single/4 x 3.5/1940-50.

Figure 2.5c-166
504/Vase/Shell Planting/7.5H/1940-46.

Figure 2.5c-168
506/Bowl/Shell/5.5H/1940-50.

95

Figure 2.5c-169
507/Vase/Shell Oval/7.5H/1940-50.

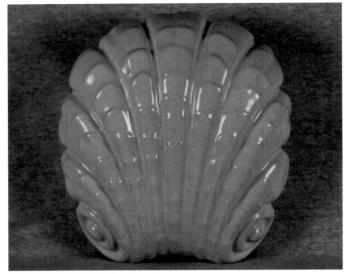

Figure 2.5c-170
508/Wall Pocket/Shell/7H/1940.

Figure 2.5c-171
509/Ashtray/Elephant/5.5D/1940-41.

Figure 2.5c-172
510/Ashtray/Donkey/5.5D/1940-41.

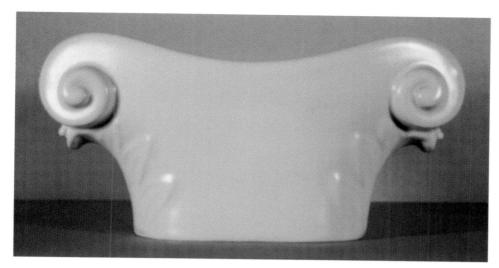

Figure 2.5c-173
511/Vase/Ionic/8L/1940-41. *Courtesy of Brian and Anita Hickok.*

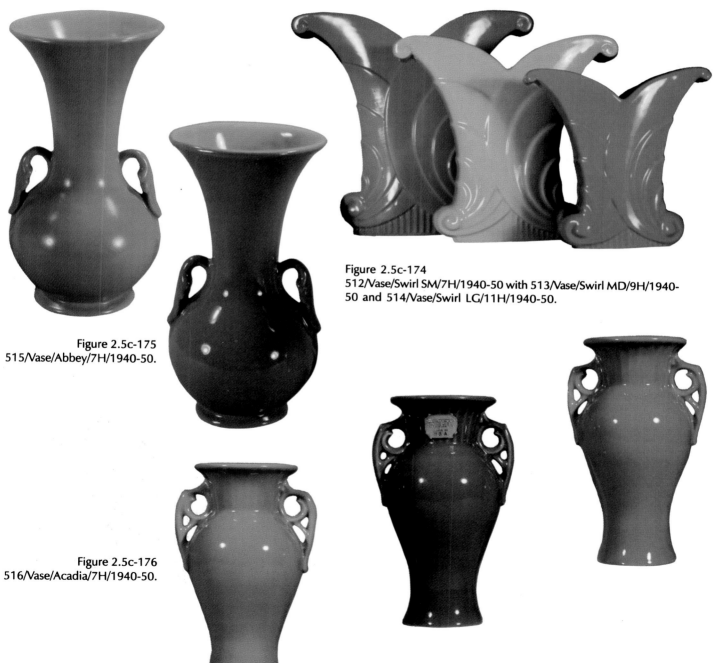

Figure 2.5c-174
512/Vase/Swirl SM/7H/1940-50 with 513/Vase/Swirl MD/9H/1940-50 and 514/Vase/Swirl LG/11H/1940-50.

Figure 2.5c-175
515/Vase/Abbey/7H/1940-50.

Figure 2.5c-176
516/Vase/Acadia/7H/1940-50.

Figure 2.5c-177
517/Vase/Arden/7H/1940-50.

Figure 2.5c-178
518/Bowl/Round
Bulb/12D/1940-
50 with 519/Bowl/
Round Bulb/9D/
1940-50 and 543/
Bowl/Round Bulb
SM/5.5D/1941-
46. *Courtesy of
Christine and
Jamie Boone.*

Figure 2.5c-179
520/Vase/Baden/9H/1940-48.

Figure 2.5c-180
521/Vase/Bali/9H/1940-41. *Courtesy of
Robert Rush.*

Figure 2.5c-181
522/Vase/Barre/9H/1940-50.

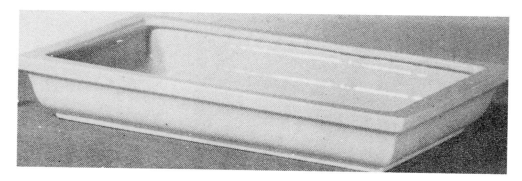

Figure 2.5c-182
523/Bowl/Han Oblong/14 x 9/1940.

Figure 2.5c-184
525/Bowl/Flare Oblong/10 x 7/1940-50. *Courtesy of Robert Rush.*

Figure 2.5c-183
524/Vase Floor/Egret LG/17.5H/1940-50 with 487/Vase/Floor/Egret
SM/14H/1939-50. When sold with Sand trap, the 524 is called a
524A Sand Jar.

Figure 2.5c-185
526/Bowl/Bulb Oblong/10 x 6/1940-50.

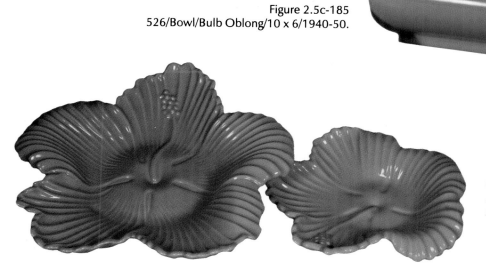

Figure 2.5c-186
527/Bowl/Hibiscus SM/10D/1941-48 with
528/Bowl/Hibiscus LG/15D/1941-49.

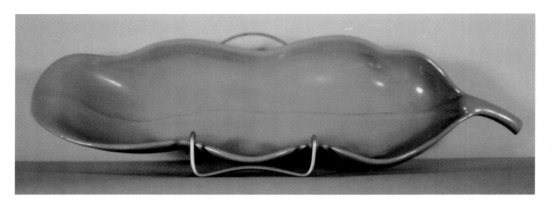

Figure 2.5c-187
529/Bowl/Ti Leaf/
16 x 5/1941-46.
*Courtesy of Brian
and Anita Hickok.*

Figure 2.5c-188
530/Bowl/
Traveler's Palm/16
x 6.5/1941-46.

Figure 2.5c-189
531/Bowl/Fleur-
De-Lis/14 x 9/
1941. *Courtesy of
Christine and
Jamie Boone.*

Figure 2.5c-190
532/Bowl/Scroll
MD/14.5L/1941-
50 center with
478/Bowl/Scroll
SM/11.5L/1939-
41 and 480/Bowl/
Scroll LG/17.5L/
1939-50. *Courtesy
of Christine and
Jamie Boone.*

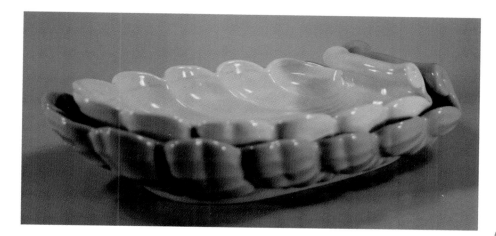

Figure 2.5c-191
533/Bowl/Shell/12L/1941-50 with 500/
Bowl/Shell LG/15L/1940-49.

Figure 2.5c-192
534/Vase/Boyne/
9H/1941-46.

Figure 2.5c-193
535/Vase/Berne/9H/1941-46.

Figure 2.5c-194
536/Bowl/Regency/9L/1941-50.

Figure 2.5c-195
537/Vase/Tassel/9H/1941.

Figure 2.5c-196
538/Urn/Wreath/
9H/1941-46,
1950.

Figure 2.5c-198
540/Bowl/Flare/
11.5 x 8/1941 at
bottom left with
541/Bowl/Oval
LG/15 x 9/1941
and 480/Bowl/
Scroll LG/17.5L/
1939-50 at
bottom right; 531/
Bowl/Fleur-De-Lis/
14 x 9/1941 and
478/Bowl/Scroll
SM/11.5L/1939-
41 in center; and
532/Bowl/Scroll
MD/14.5L/1941-
50 at top.

Figure 2.5c-197
539/Urn/Regency/7H/1941. *Courtesy of Robert Rush.*

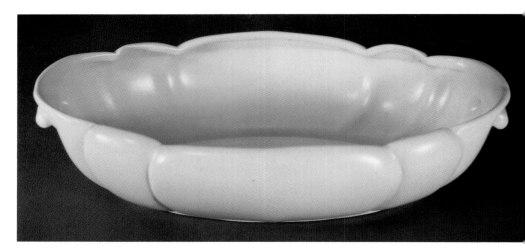

Figure 2.5c-199
541/Bowl/Oval
LG/15 x 9/1941.
*Courtesy of
Christine and
Jamie Boone.*

Figure 2.5c-200
542/Bowl/Oval
Bulb LG/15 x 9/
1941-50. *Courtesy
of Christine and
Jamie Boone.*

Figure 2.5c-201
543D/Box/Geranium/3.25H/1947 Note,
the bottom was sold as 543/Bowl/Round
Bulb SM/5.5D/1941-46—see 518 and
519.

Figure 2.5c-202
544/Bowl/
Streamliner SM/9
x 6/1942-50 with
545/Bowl/
Streamliner MD/8
x 11/1941-50 and
546/Bowl/
Streamliner LG/9 x
14.5/1941-46.
*Courtesy of
Christine and
Jamie Boone.*

Figure 2.5c-203
547/Bowl/Irregular/7 x 10/1941-46.
Courtesy of Brian and Anita Hickok.

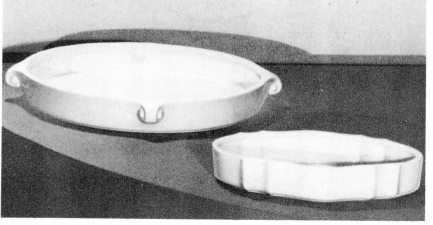

Figure 2.5c-204
548/Bowl/Round LG/14D/1941 with 547/
Bowl/Irregular/7 x 10/1941-46.

Figure 2.5c-205
549/Cookie Jar/Hippo/8H x 7D/1941-47.

Figure 2.5c-206
550/Vase/Fluted/11H/1941-50.

Figure 2.5c-207
551/Ashtray/
Octagonal /7SQ/
1941-46. *Courtesy
of Christine and
Jamie Boone.*

Figure 2.5c-208
552/Vase/Squatty/8.5D/1941-48.

Figure 2.5c-209
553/Vase/Grecian/13H/1941-46.

Figure 2.5c-210
554/Vase/Ribbed/9H/1941-46.

Figure 2.5c-211
555/Ashtray/Round/8D/1941-46. *Courtesy of Robert Rush.*

Figure 2.5c-212
556/Vase/Large/12.5H/1941-46. *Courtesy of Robert Rush.*

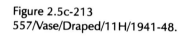

Figure 2.5c-213
557/Vase/Draped/11H/1941-48.

Figure 2.5c-215
561/Cookie Jar/Baby/11H x 8D/1941-46.

Figure 2.5c-214
558/Cache Pot SM/4.75/1947
with 559/Cache Pot MD/5.5H/
1947-48 560/Cache Pot LG/
6.5H/1947 and 560D/Cache Pot
LG/6.5H/1942. *Courtesy of
Robert Rush.*

Figure 2.5c-216
561-71D/Cookie Jar/Special/8H/1941-42.

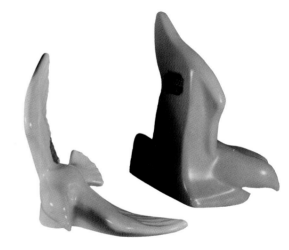

Figure 2.5c-218
563/Urn/9H/1947-48. *Courtesy of Christine and Jamie Boone.*

Figure 2.5c-217
562/Animal Figure/Gull/5H/1942 with
pink 305/Bookends/Seagull/6H/1934-46.

Figure 2.5c-220
565/
Cornucopia/
High/7H/
1947-48.
*Courtesy of
Christine and
Jamie
Boone.*

Figure 2.5c-219
564/Bowl/Scallop/11L/1942-50.

Figure 2.5c-221
566/Vase/Scallop/9H/1947-48.

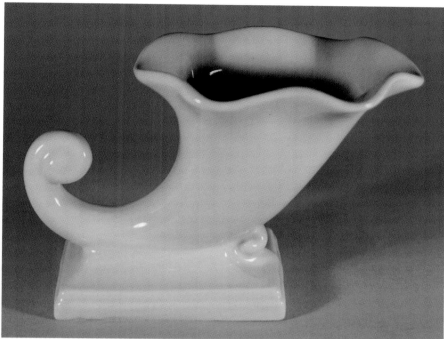

Figure 2.5c-224
569/Cornucopia/Low/8L/1947-48.

Figure 2.5c-222
567/Vase/Low/5H/1947. *Courtesy of Christine and Jamie Boone.*

Figure 2.5c-225
570/Window Box/10L/1947-50.

Figure 2.5c-226
571/Animal Figure/Goose Sitting/5H/1942-47.

Figure 2.5c-223
568/Compote/Mint/6D/1942-47 at left with 638/Compote/4H/1948-50 at right.

Figure 2.5c-227
572/Animal
Figure/Pelican/5H/
1942-46. *Courtesy
of Brian and Anita
Hickok.*

Figure 2.5c-228
573D/Animal
Figure/Penguin/
5H/1947.
*Courtesy of Brian
and Anita Hickok.*

Figure 2.5c-229
574/Animal
Figure/Heron/
5.25H/1942-46.

Figure 2.5c-230
575/Candleholder/Double/5H/1942-50.

Figure 2.5c-231
576/Window Box/LG/12.25L/1947-50.

Figure 2.5c-232
577/Vase/Pillow/7H/1947-50.

Figure 2.5c-233
578/Candleholder/Victory Boat. *Courtesy of Robert Rush.*

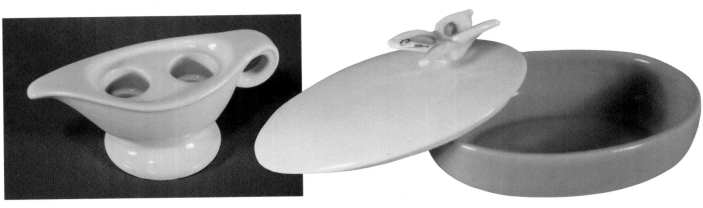

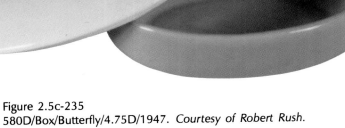

Figure 2.5c-234
579/Candleholder/Aladdin Lamp.
Courtesy of Christine and Jamie Boone.

Figure 2.5c-235
580D/Box/Butterfly/4.75D/1947. *Courtesy of Robert Rush.*

Figure 2.5c-236
581/Cornucopia/
Double/8.25H/
1947-48.

Figure 2.5c-237
582D/Basket/Flower/8H/1947-48.
Courtesy of Brian and Anita Hickok.

Figure 2.5c-238
583/Cornucopia/
Triple/9D/1947-
48.

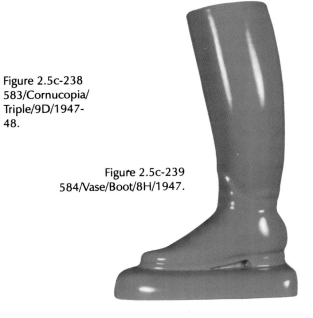

Figure 2.5c-239
584/Vase/Boot/8H/1947.

Figure 2.5c-240
585D/Box/Rosebud/4.5D/1947-48.

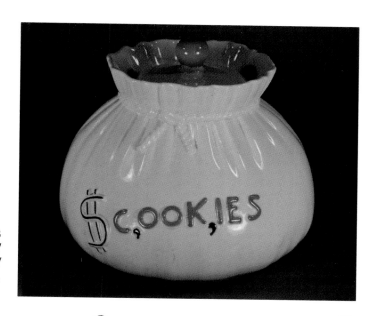

Figure 2.5c-243
588D/Cookie Jar/
Money Bag/7.5H/
1947-50.

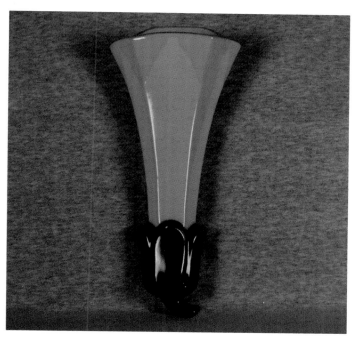

Figure 2.5c-241
586D/Wall Vase/
Calla/9H/1947-48.

Figure 2.5c-242
587/Wall Bracket/Cherub/7.5H/1947.

Figure 2.5c-244
589/Wall Bracket/
Acanthus/7H/
1947.

Figure 2.5c-245
590D/Wall Pocket/
Ivy/7H/1947.
*Courtesy of Robert
Rush.*

Figure 2.5c-246
591/Vase/Pleat/
10H/1947-48.

Figure 2.5c-247
592/Bowl/Low Oval/10.5L/1947-50.
Courtesy of Christine and Jamie Boone.

Figure 2.5c-248
593/Vase/Bow
Knot/9H/1947-48.

Figure 2.5c-249
594/Vase/Hour
Glass/9H/1947.

Figure 2.5c-250
595/Bookend/Quill Pen/8.25/1947-48.

Figure 2.5c-251
596D/Vase/Sea Horse/8H/1947-48.
Courtesy of Christine and Jamie Boone.

Figure 2.5c-252
597/Vase/Trumpet/9H/1947. *Courtesy of
Christine and Jamie Boone.*

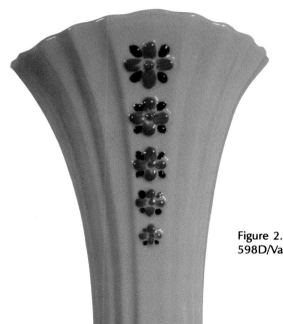

Figure 2.5c-253
598D/Vase/Rosette/7.25H/1947-48.

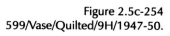

Figure 2.5c-254
599/Vase/Quilted/9H/1947-50.

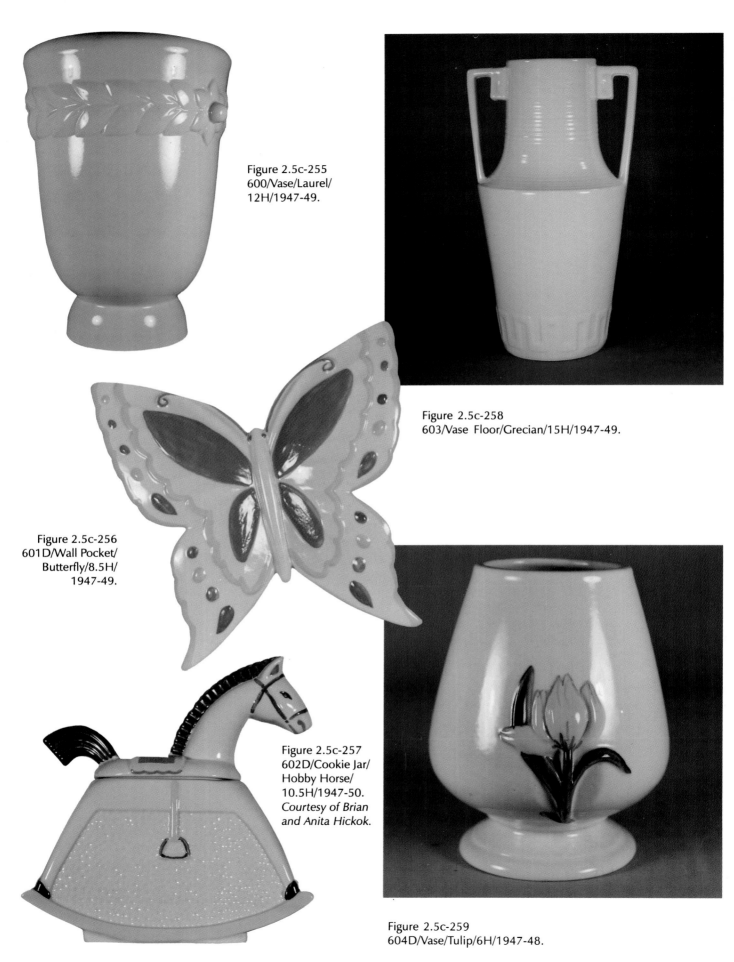

Figure 2.5c-255
600/Vase/Laurel/
12H/1947-49.

Figure 2.5c-258
603/Vase Floor/Grecian/15H/1947-49.

Figure 2.5c-256
601D/Wall Pocket/
Butterfly/8.5H/
1947-49.

Figure 2.5c-257
602D/Cookie Jar/
Hobby Horse/
10.5H/1947-50.
*Courtesy of Brian
and Anita Hickok.*

Figure 2.5c-259
604D/Vase/Tulip/6H/1947-48.

Figure 2.5c-260
605D/Animal Figure/Kangaroo/7H/1947.

Figure 2.5c-261
606/Jar/Elephant/9.75H/1947.

Figure 2.5c-262
607D/Box/Candy
Cane/4.5H/1947-
48.

Figure 2.5c-263
608/Box/Elephant/6L/1947-48.

Figure 2.5c-264
609D/Jar/Pelican/6.5H/1947.

Figure 2.5c-265
610/Bowl/Shell Deep/9D/1947-48.
Courtesy of Robert Rush.

Figure 2.5c-266
611D/Cookie Jar/Jack-in-the-Box/11H/
1947-49. *Courtesy of Brian and Anita
Hickok.*

Figure 2.5c-267
612/Box/Lily Tray/9.5L/1947. *Courtesy of
Robert Rush.*

Figure 2.5c-268
613/Vase Floor/
Grecian Pitcher/
15H/1947.

Figure 2.5c-271
616D/Vase/Cactus/6.5H/1947-50.

617 thru 624 mold numbers were never assigned.

Figure 2.5c-269
614/Candleholder/Candle Reflector/6.5H/1947.

Figure 2.5c-270
615/Ashtray/Chic/5.5D/1947-48.

Figure 2.5c-272
625/Vase/Ribbed/6.5H/1948.

Figure 2.5c-273
626/Vase/Taper/6H/1948-49.

Figure 2.5c-276
629D/Vase/Poppy/6.5H/1948-49.

Figure 2.5c-274
627/Cache Pot/6H/1948-49. *Courtesy of Robert Rush.*

Figure 2.5c-275
628D/Vase/Iris/
8H/1948-49.
*Courtesy of Brian
and Anita Hickok.*

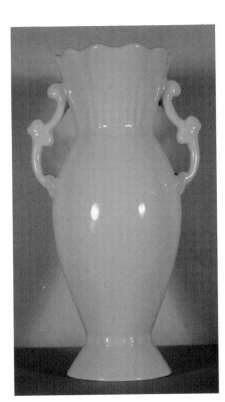

Figure 2.5c-277
630/Vase/
Handled/9H/
1948-49. *Courtesy
of Brian and Anita
Hickok.*

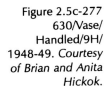

Figure 2.5c-278
631/Vase/Square/
8H/1948-49.

Figure 2.5c-279
632/Vase/Anchor/
7.5H/1948-49.
*Courtesy of Brian
and Anita Hickok.*

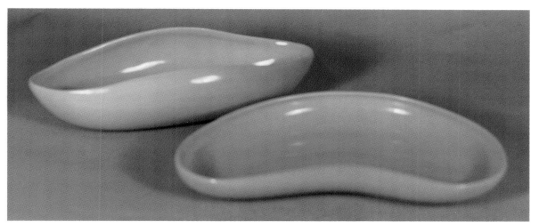

Figure 2.5c-280
633/Bowl/Tray/
10L/1948-50 in
foreground with
645/Bowl/
Contour/10.75L/
1948-50. *Courtesy
of Robert Rush.*

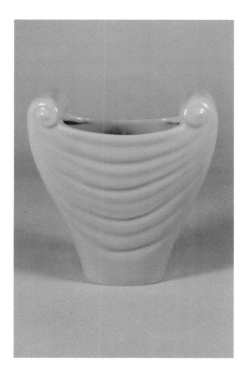

Figure 2.5c-281
634/Vase/
Heirloom/6.5H/
1948. *Courtesy of
Robert Rush.*

Figure 2.5c-282
635/Vase/Pocket/
6H/1948.
*Courtesy of Brian
and Anita Hickok.*

Figure 2.5c-283
636D/Vase/Triangular/6.25H/1948.

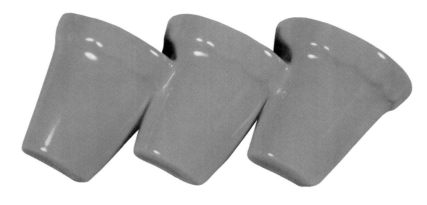

Figure 2.5c-287
640/Wall Pocket/Triad/8 x 5.5/1948-50.

Figure 2.5c-284
637/Vase/Oblong/
9H/1948-50.
*Courtesy of
Knoxville Mu-
seum.*

Figure 2.5c-286
639/Vase/Calla/
8.5H/1948.
*Courtesy of
Christine and
Jamie Boone.*

Figure 2.5c-285
638/Compote/4H/
1948-50 at left
with 568/
Compote/Mint/
6D/1942-47 at
right.

Figure 2.5c-288
641/Bowl/Whirl/
6.5H/1948.
*Courtesy of Robert
Rush.*

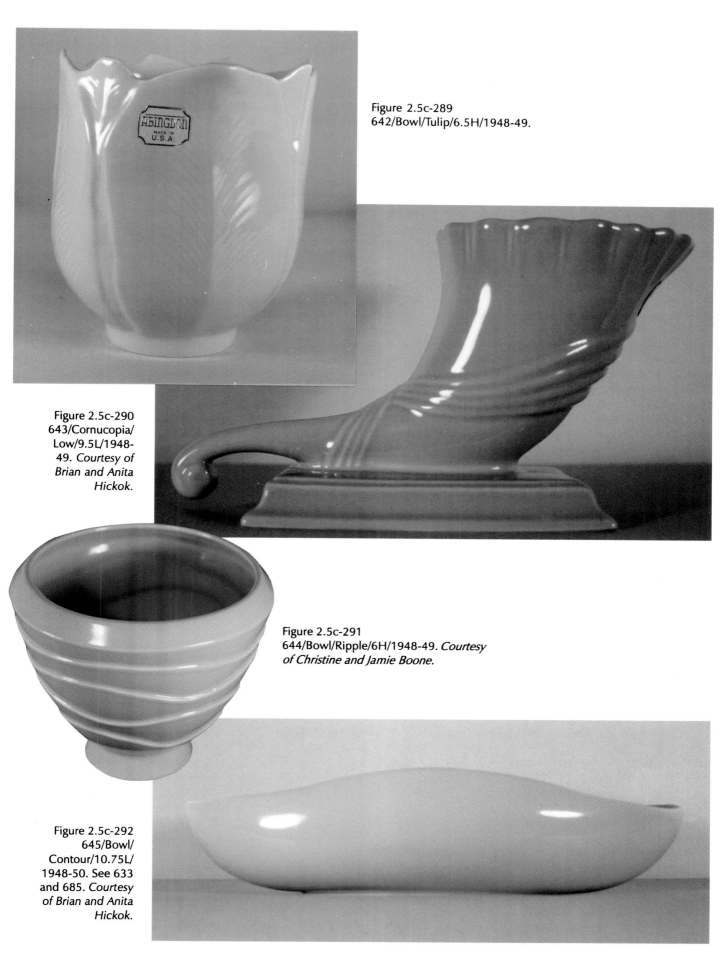

Figure 2.5c-289
642/Bowl/Tulip/6.5H/1948-49.

Figure 2.5c-290
643/Cornucopia/
Low/9.5L/1948-
49. *Courtesy of
Brian and Anita
Hickok.*

Figure 2.5c-291
644/Bowl/Ripple/6H/1948-49. *Courtesy
of Christine and Jamie Boone.*

Figure 2.5c-292
645/Bowl/
Contour/10.75L/
1948-50. See 633
and 685. *Courtesy
of Brian and Anita
Hickok.*

Figure 2.5c-293
646/Cornucopia/High/7H/1948-49.

Figure 2.5c-294
647/Urn/Tall/13.5/1948-50. *Courtesy of Robert Rush.*

Figure 2.5c-295
648/Wall Vase/Acanthus/8.75H/1948-50.

Figure 2.5c-296
649/Wall Bracket/Acanthus/8.75H/1948.

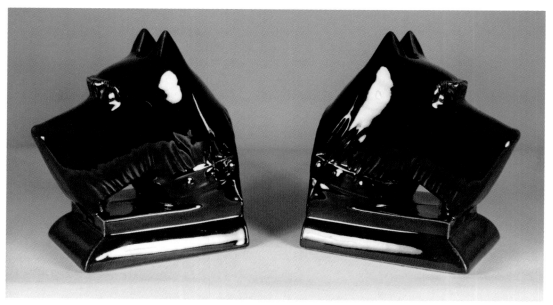

Figure 2.5c-297
650/Bookend/
Scotty/7.5H/1948.

Figure 2.5c-298
651D/Cookie Jar/Choo Choo/7.5H/1948-50. *Courtesy of Brian and Anita Hickok.*

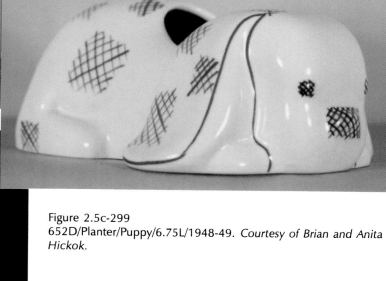

Figure 2.5c-299
652D/Planter/Puppy/6.75L/1948-49. *Courtesy of Brian and Anita Hickok.*

Figure 2.5c-300
653D/Cookie Jar/Clock/9H/1948-50.

Figure 2.5c-301
654/Vase/Tulip/6.5H/1948-49.

Figure 2.5c-302
655D/Planter/Dutch Shoe/5L/1948.

Figure 2.5c-303 656/Planter/ Square/3.5H/ 1948-50. *Courtesy of Brian and Anita Hickok.*

Figure 2.5c-304 657/Animal Figure/Swordfish/ 4.5H/1948-50. *Courtesy of Brian and Anita Hickok.*

Figure 2.5c-305 658/Bowl/Ribbed/ 10L/1948-50. *Courtesy of Christine and Jamie Boone.*

Figure 2.5c-306 659/Vase/Hackney/8.5H/1948-49.

Figure 2.5c-307
660/Ashtray/Leaf/5.5D/1948-50.

Figure 2.5c-308
661/Animal Figure/Swan/3.75H/1948-50. *Courtesy of Brian and Anita Hickok.*

Figure 2.5c-309
662D/Cookie Jar/Miss Muffet/11H/1949-50. *Courtesy of Brian and Anita Hickok.*

Figure 2.5c-310
663D/Cookie Jar/
Humpty Dumpty/
10.5H/1949-50.
*Courtesy of Brian
and Anita Hickok.*

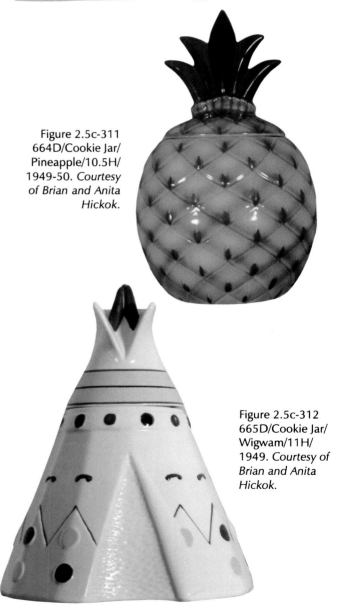

Figure 2.5c-311
664D/Cookie Jar/
Pineapple/10.5H/
1949-50. *Courtesy
of Brian and Anita
Hickok.*

Figure 2.5c-312
665D/Cookie Jar/
Wigwam/11H/
1949. *Courtesy of
Brian and Anita
Hickok.*

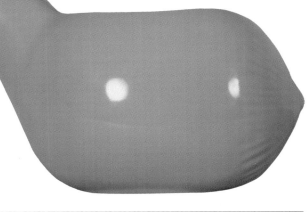

Figure 2.5c-314
667/Planter/Gourd/5.5H/1949-50.

Figure 2.5c-313
666D/Jam Set/4 Piece/3.5H/1949-50.
Courtesy of Knoxville Museum.

Figure 2.5c-315
668D/Planter/Daffodil/5.25H/1949.

Figure 2.5c-316
669/Planter/Donkey/7.5H/1949-50.

Figure 2.5c-317
670/Planter/Pooch/4H/1949-50.

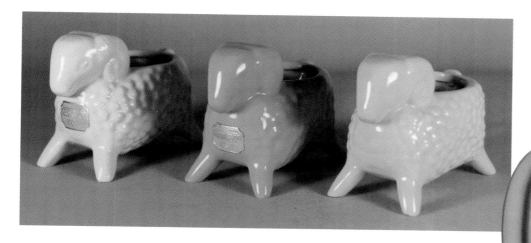

Figure 2.5c-318
671/Planter/Ram/4H/1949-50.

Figure 2.5c-321
674D/Cookie Jar/Pumpkin/8H/1949-50.
Courtesy of Brian and Anita Hickok.

Figure 2.5c-322
675D/Wall Vase/Match Box/5.5H/1949-50.

Figure 2.5c-319
672/Planter/Fawn/5H/1949-50.

Figure 2.5c-320
673/Planter/Burro/
4.5H/1949-50.
*Courtesy of
Christine and
Jamie Boone.*

Figure 2.5c-323
676D/Wall Vase/
Book/6.5H/1949.

Figure 2.5c-324
677D/Cookie Jar/Daisy/8H/1949-50.

Figure 2.5c-326
679/Grease Jar/Daisy/4.5H/1949-50.

Figure 2.5c-325
678D/Cookie Jar/Windmill/10.5H/1949. *Courtesy of Brian and Anita Hickok.*

Figure 2.5c-327
680/Salt & Pepper/Daisy/4H/1949-50.

Figure 2.5c-328
681/Sugar Bowl/3H/1949-50.

Figure 2.5c-329
682/Cream Pitcher/Daisy/1949-50.

Figure 2.5c-330
683/Tea Pot/Daisy/6.25H/1949-50.

Figure 2.5c-331
684/Bowl/Crescent/5W/1949. *Courtesy of Christine and Jamie Boone.*

Figure 2.5c-332
685/Bowl/Ribbed LG/13.75L/1949-50 at right in green; 686/Bowl/Contour LG/13.25L/1949; 688/Candleholder/Ribbed/1.75H/1949 at right in green; 689/Candleholder/Contour/1.75H/1949 at left in blue. *Courtesy of Robert Rush.*

Figure 2.5c-333
687/Bowl/Planter/5SQ/1949-50. *Courtesy of Christine and Jamie Boone.*

Figure 2.5c-336
692D/Cookie Jar/Witch/11.5H/1950.

Figure 2.5c-334
690D/Range Set/Daisy/3 pieces/1949-50.

Figure 2.5c-337
693D/Cookie Jar/Little Girl/9.5H/
1950. *Courtesy of Brian and Anita Hickok.*

Figure 2.5c-335
691D/Tea Set/Daisy/3 pieces/1949-50.

Figure 2.5c-338
694D/Cookie Jar/Bo Peep/12H/1950. *Courtesy of Brian and Anita Hickok.*

Figure 2.5c-340
696D/Cookie Jar/Three Bears/8.75H/1950.

Figure 2.5c-339
695D/Cookie Jar/Mother Goose/12H/1950. *Courtesy of Brian and Anita Hickok.*

Figure 2.5c-341
697D/Cookie Jar/Floral/Plaid/8.5H/1950. *Courtesy of Brian and Anita Hickok.*

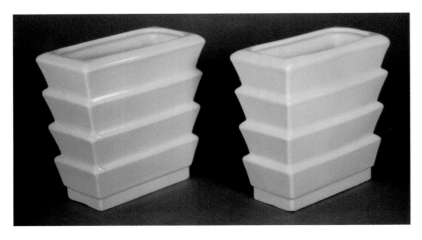

Figure 2.5c-342
698/Vase/Chinese Terrace/6H/1950.

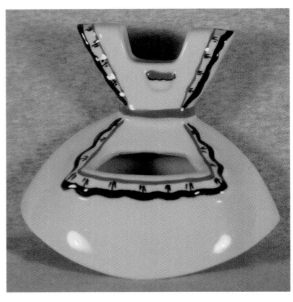

Figure 2.5c-343
699D/Wall Vase/Apron/6H/1950.

Figure 2.5c-344
700D/Bowl/Pineapple/14.75L/1950.

Figure 2.5c-345
701/Planter/
Chinese Square/
4.75H/1950.

Figure 2.5c-346
702D/String Holder/Chinese Face/5.5H/
1950. *Courtesy of Robert Rush.*

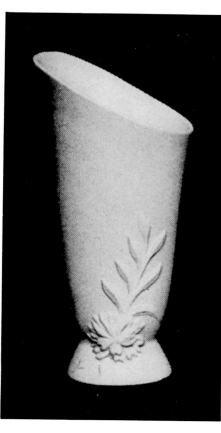

Figure 2.5c-347
703/Vase/Slant
Top/9.5H/1950.

Figure 2.5c-349
705/Vase/Modern/
8H/1950.
*Courtesy of
Christine and
Jamie Boone.*

Figure 2.5c-350
706/Vase/Oak Leaf/9.25H/1950. The blue
vase on the right is Abingdon, the yellow
on the left is not.

Figure 2.5c-348
704/Planter /Gazelle/4.75H/1950.

Figure 2.5c-351
707/Bowl/Cradle Planter/6.5L/1950.

Figure 2.5c-352
708/Vase/Square Leaf/9H/1950. *Courtesy of Brian and Anita Hickok.*

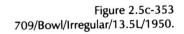

Figure 2.5c-353
709/Bowl/Irregular/13.5L/1950.

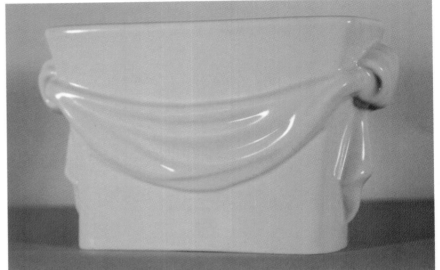

Figure 2.5c-354
710/Planter/Drape/7L/1950. *Courtesy of Brian and Anita Hickok.*

Figure 2.5c-355
711/Wall Vase/Carriage Lamp/10H/1950.

Figure 2.5c-357
713/Bowl/Star Console/10D/1950.
Courtesy of Christine and Jamie Boone.

Figure 2.5c-358
714/
Candleholder/Star/
4.25/1950.
*Courtesy of
Christine and
Jamie Boone.*

Figure 2.5c-360
717/Vase/Mrs. Bidwell/1950. *Courtesy of Robert Rush.*

Figure 2.5c-359
715D/Plate/Bamboo Console/10.5D/1950 with 716D/
Candleholder/Bamboo Square/3.5SQ/1950. *Courtesy of Brian and
Anita Hickok.*

Figure 2.5c-361
718/Vase/Basket Weave/1950. *Courtesy of Robert Rush.*

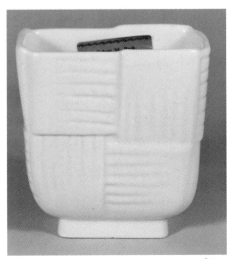

Figure 2.5c-362
719/
Candleholder/
Redesign of 479/
1950 with 720/
Bowl/Redesign of
480/18L/1950.
*Courtesy of Robert
Rush.*

Figure 2.5c-363
721/Window Box/12.5L/1950. *Courtesy
of Robert Rush.*

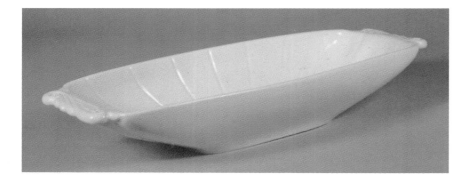

Figure 2.5c-364
722/Bowl/Oblong Fruit/14.5L/1950.
Courtesy of Robert Rush.

Figure 2.5c-365
723/Not Documented. Not certain that this number was ever assigned.

Figure 2.5c-366
724/Wall Pocket/
Leaf/10 x 5.5L/
1950. *Courtesy of
Robert Rush.*

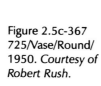

Figure 2.5c-367
725/Vase/Round/
1950. *Courtesy of
Robert Rush.*

Figure 2.5c-368
726/Planter/Cart/5 x 5SQ/1950. *Courtesy of Betty Perry. Photo taken by Tom Foley of Midwest Photo.*

Figure 2.5c-369
727/Vase/Mrs. Andrews/1950.

Figure 2.5c-370
728/Not Documented. Not certain this number was ever assigned.

Figure 2.5c-371
729/Window Box/ Scroll End//1950. No Photo available.

Figure 2.5c-372
730/Vase/Modern Bud/8.5H/1950. *Courtesy of Christine and Jamie Boone.*

Figure 2.5c-373
731/Not Documented. Not certain this number was ever assigned.

Figure 2.5c-374
732/Planter/Square Fluted/6SQ/1950. No Photo available.

Figure 2.5c-375
733/Bowl/Right Angle/5 x 5 x 5/1950. No Photo available.

Figure 2.5c-376
734/Candleholder/Cube/2.5SQ/1950. No Photo available.

Figure 2.5c-377
735/Not Documented. Not certain this number was ever assigned.

Figure 2.5d-1
861/Egyptian vase/
Several pre-
artware era
designs.

Figure 2.5d-2
A Spittoon of pre-artware vintage.

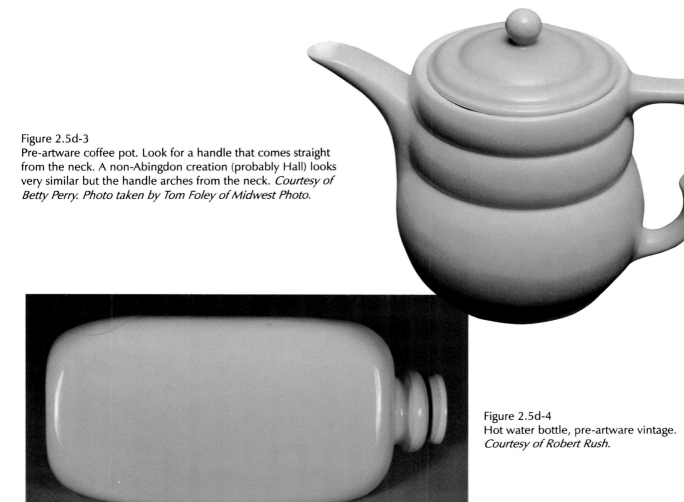

Figure 2.5d-3
Pre-artware coffee pot. Look for a handle that comes straight from the neck. A non-Abingdon creation (probably Hall) looks very similar but the handle arches from the neck. *Courtesy of Betty Perry. Photo taken by Tom Foley of Midwest Photo.*

Figure 2.5d-4
Hot water bottle, pre-artware vintage.
Courtesy of Robert Rush.

Figure 2.5d-5
Little Boy with Sand Pail. Date not certain, but believed to be during the artware era.

Figure 2.5d-6
Buddha, same vintage as Little Boy with Sand Pail.

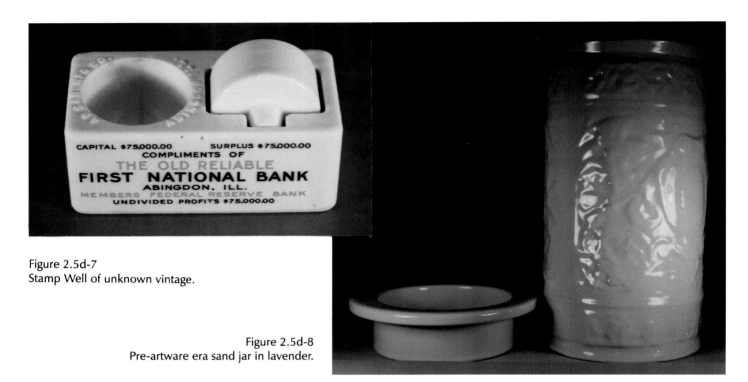

Figure 2.5d-7
Stamp Well of unknown vintage.

Figure 2.5d-8
Pre-artware era sand jar in lavender.

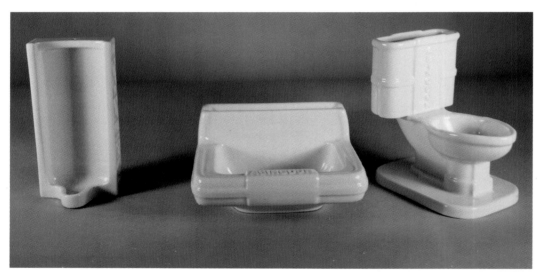

Figure 2.5d-9
Novelty items which are replicas of the plumbingware made by Abingdon Sanitary Manufacturing Company.

Figure 2.5d-10
Desk Set of the artware era.

Figure 2.5d-11
Soda fountain jars of unknown vintage.

Figure 2.5d-12
Indian figures of artware era. Not
production items. *Courtesy of Elaine
Westover.*

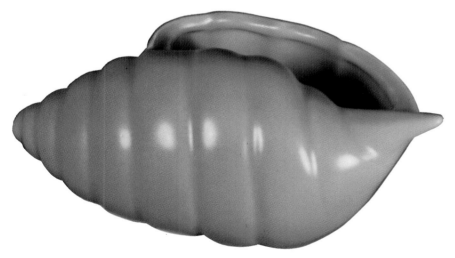

Figure 2.5d-13
Conch Shell. Late artware piece.

Figure 2.5d-14
"Bottoms Up" shot glass. Post artware era
piece. This piece was reported by the
owner to have been made decades after
the close of the Artware Division.
Courtesy of Elaine Westover.

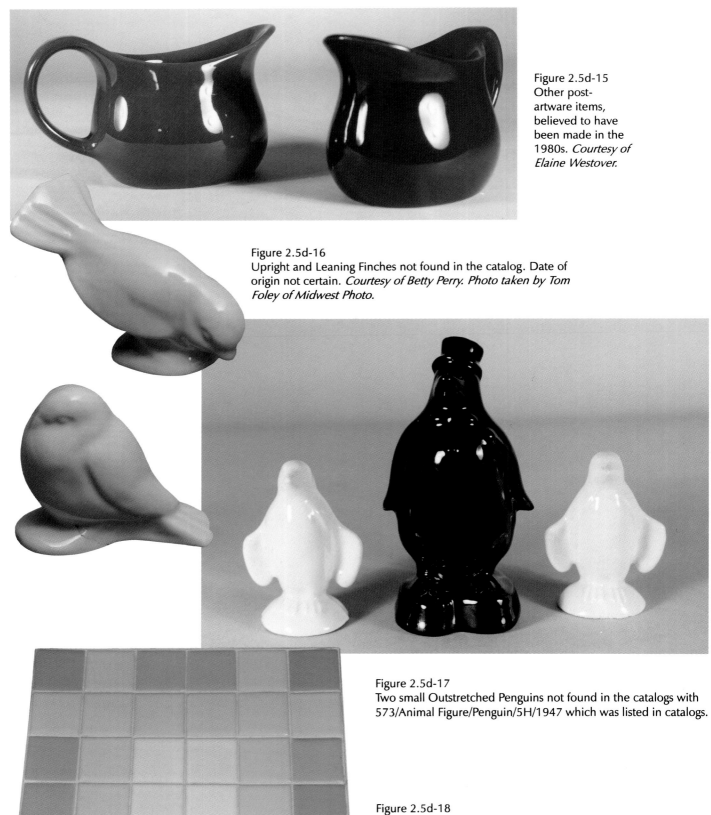

Figure 2.5d-15
Other post-
artware items,
believed to have
been made in the
1980s. *Courtesy of
Elaine Westover.*

Figure 2.5d-16
Upright and Leaning Finches not found in the catalog. Date of
origin not certain. *Courtesy of Betty Perry. Photo taken by Tom
Foley of Midwest Photo.*

Figure 2.5d-17
Two small Outstretched Penguins not found in the catalogs with
573/Animal Figure/Penguin/5H/1947 which was listed in catalogs.

Figure 2.5d-18
Believed to be a group of test tiles once used by Lloyd Petrie,
Ceramic Engineer for the Abingdon Pottery.

3.1 OVERVIEW

One aspect of Abingdon's artware most frequently remarked on by dealers and collectors alike is the color of the glazes. Photos in the 3.1 series of figures provide a sampling of Abingdon's colors and glaze textures. Six color "groups" attract premium prices: all black, brown, grey, dark blue, dark red, and orange colors. Of these, black gloss (Black) is the most easily found, followed by metallic black (Gunmetal Black), then the dark red (Royal Red/Dubonnet—one color with two names not to be confused with a medium red called Sudan Red) and the dark blue (Riviera Blue/Royal Blue—three shades of deep blue with two names) colors being equally hard to find. The browns (Copper Brown—several variations in darkness and iridescence) and greys (Copenhagen Gray and Grey—two distinct colors) are hard to find and orange (Fire Red) is rarest of all referred to above.

All of these colors are the earliest of Abingdon creations, as are three other colors worthy of note: Regency Green; Dawn Blue; Lake Green. One post-WWII color, Sierra, a light lush blue, is also a very desirable color. Finally, several colors of unknown vintage are also worthy of note: the iridescent mother-of-pearl color, lavender, weathered green, and mottled green.

The exact number of colors used on Abingdon Pottery artware has been the subject of much discussion. There were approximately 45 separate colors listed in the catalogs. John Lewis estimated that almost 150 colors were developed for artware which suggests that many non-catalog colors were developed and, indeed, many have been found.

The Pottery was aggressive in developing new colors. There was a color "palette" for every catalog. Each palette offered 6 to 10 different colors for standard pieces with additional colors being offered for specialty items

(Gunmetal Black being the most frequent of these specialty colors followed by Dubonnet and Royal Blue). New colors were offered once and sometimes twice a year.

Each color in the catalogs had a color code, a color name, and most colors had a description—some of the *Classic*, *LaFleur*, and specialty colors were presented without descriptions. Each color code was three characters long with the first character almost always being the same letter as the first letter in the name of the color family it represented: B for blue, G for green, R for red, W for white, Y for yellow, and D for the "Dark" family or all colors of black, brown, and grey (B and G being already used for the blue and green families). There were three color codes beginning with letters not the same as the first letter of the family to which they belonged: two in the red family (T10 for Sudan Red and T20 for Autumn Peach) and one in the green family (C10 for Royal Chartreuse). The last two characters of the three-character code were always numbers identifying individual colors within a color family.

The information in the catalogs was fairly straightforward until the introduction of more than one color palette per catalog. From the Spring of 1938 through the Spring of 1941, double palettes were published: one "Standard" palette for the standard line of products and another "Classic" palette for the newly introduced *Classic* and *LaFleur* lines of artware. It was at this point that the association of color codes, names, and descriptions became erratic, contradictory, and confusing. In addition, specialty items such as the three water jugs (200-202), the refrigerator water jug (113), and the large garden vases (G1 and G2) often had their own palettes. Thus, the contradictory data in the catalogs make positive identification of some colors impossible.

Figure 3.1-1
Bell Crater Urn (309) in Copper Brown;
Coupe service plate (343) in Royal Blue;
Arden vase (517) in Two-Tone (Gloss
Black and Jonquil Yellow); Han vase (312)
in Fire Red; Beta *Classic* vase (106) in
Dubonnet; Capri vase (351) in Regency
Green; and Kneeling Nude (3903) in
Gunmetal Black. *Courtesy of Robert Rush.*

Figure 3.1-2
Trojan Head vase or bookend (499) in
Jasmine Yellow; Ring vase (318) and
Fairfield vase (307) in Lake Green;
Modern vase #1 (310) in Dawn Blue;
Coupe soup bowl (338) in Fire Red; and
Shell Cornucopia (449) in pink with
Platinum. *Courtesy of Robert Rush.*

Figure 3.1-3
Refrigerator water jug (113) in Royal Blue
(compare this "Cobalt" color to softer
cclor of the Coupe service plate (343) in
Figure 3.1-1); Trojan Head (449) in Black;
Blackamour (497) in hand-painted variety.
Courtesy of Elaine Westover.

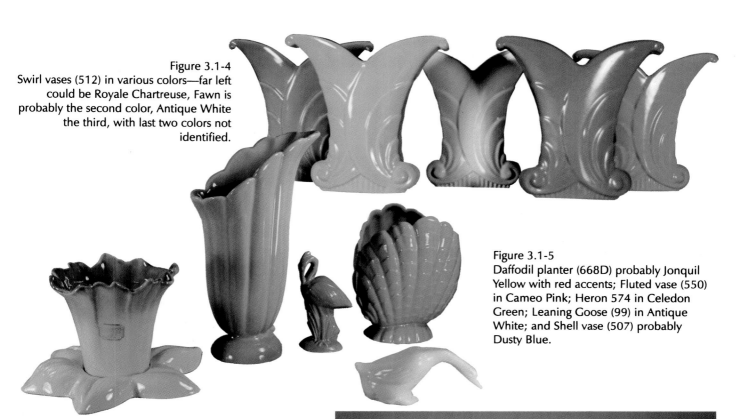

Figure 3.1-4
Swirl vases (512) in various colors—far left could be Royale Chartreuse, Fawn is probably the second color, Antique White the third, with last two colors not identified.

Figure 3.1-5
Daffodil planter (668D) probably Jonquil Yellow with red accents; Fluted vase (550) in Cameo Pink; Heron 574 in Celedon Green; Leaning Goose (99) in Antique White; and Shell vase (507) probably Dusty Blue.

Figure 3.1-6
Two large Lace Cuffed vases (446) one in Ariel Blue, the other in Yellow Chartreuse.

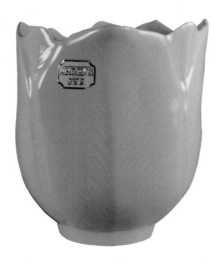

Figure 3.1-7
Swedish Goblet (322) in Lemon Yellow—one of the earliest pieces in one of the earliest colors; Tulip bowl (642) in Sierra—one of the latest pieces in one of the latest colors. Compare these two gloss colors to the matt colors in Figure 3.1-6.

3.2 COLOR DICTIONARY

(a) The Blue Family

ARIEL BLUE(B14)/1939-40 (Figure 3.2-1): This color appeared in four catalogs (Spring of 1939 through Fall of 1940) with the following description: "a waxy matt turquoise coloring." This color also had the same color code as the color named Turquoise (B14) which was offered in 1938 on *Classic* and *LaFleur* lines of pottery only. Turquoise (B14) was never advertised in the catalogs again after the appearance of Ariel Blue (B14). See Figure 3.2-9 for an example of Turquoise (B14).

COOL BLUE (B23)/1942-48 (Figure 3.2-2): This color appeared in three catalogs (Spring 1942, 1947, and 1948) with the same code of B23 and the description: "A light toned soft dusty blue in smooth matt texture." Cool Blue, Celedon Green and Cameo Pink were used on the bodies of the Starflower Collection introduced in 1942.

DAWN BLUE (B11)/1934-38 (Figure 3.2-3): This color appeared in the first eight catalogs (Fall of 1934 to Fall of 1938) without change in code or description: "A delicate turquoise in waxy matt texture—as true a turquoise as the gem's own name."

Figure 3.2-1
Ariel Blue on Trojan Head bookend/vase to the left. See Figure 3.2-9 for example of Turquoise which had the same color code (B14) as Ariel Blue.

Figure 3.2-2
Cool Blue Starflower cache pot.

Figure 3.2-3
Dawn Blue with Gunmetal Black.
Courtesy of Robert Rush.

DELFT BLUE (B10)/1939; DUSTY BLUE (B10)/1940 (Figure 3.2-4): Delft Blue (B10) appeared in only two catalogs (Spring and Fall of 1939) with the cryptic description: "A strong gray-blue gloss." Was offered on the *LaFleur* and *Classic* line only. Dusty Blue (B10) had the same code but was never given a description.

FROST BLUE (B18)/1941 (Figure 3.2-5): This color appeared in only two catalogs (Spring and Fall of 1941) with the description: "A light toned soft dusty blue."

Figure 3.2-4
Delft Blue *Classic* vase (120/10H/1947-49).

Figure 3.2-5
Small (Frost Blue) and Large (probably Golden Yellow) *Classic* console bowls (125/11 x 6.25 and 127/14 x 6.5 respectively) with matching candlesticks (126/2 x 3.5 inches). *Courtesy of Robert Rush.*

Figure 3.2-6
Two Royal Blue shades, the softer blue and the more dramatic gloss color often referred to today as "Cobalt Blue." *Courtesy of Elaine Westover.*

RIVIERA BLUE (B12)/1934; ROYAL BLUE (B12 & B15)/1935-47 (Figures 3.2-6 and 7): The color name Riviera Blue (B12) appeared only in the Fall of 1934 with the description: "A semi-gloss dark blue with great depth of color." Royal Blue (B12) appeared in the next catalog with the same code and description and remained through the Spring of 1936 but did not appear again until it was offered on specialty items in the Fall of 1938 with the different code of B15. Even though Royal Blue did change color codes from B12 to B15, the description did not change until later and then only slightly. Royal Blue (B15) was last listed in the 1947 catalog.

Figure 3.2-7
A third shade of Royal Blue. Compare to Figure 3.2-6.

SIERRA (B34)/1948-50 (Figure 3.2-8): This color appeared in the last three catalogs (1948 through 1950) with the description: "A rich, new light blue of gorgeous luster." This was one of the most beautiful of the post-WWII colors, having an unusually rich liquid glaze. One way to isolate this color is to find any of the Floral vases (mold numbers 176-181) in a blue color. These vases were made only in 1950 and the only blue used that year—according to the catalogs—was Sierra.

Figure 3.2-8
Sierra Blue on Square vase (631/8H/1948-49). This blue is one of the most outstanding of the post-WWII color creations.

TURQUOISE (B14)/1938 (Figure 3.2-9): This color appeared in both catalogs for the year 1938 and was offered on the *LaFleur* and *Classic* lines only. There was no description of the color provided in either of these catalogs. It has the same color code as Ariel Blue (B14).

Figure 3.2-9
Turquoise Delta shaped *Classic* vase on the left with Ariel Blue Trojan Head vase on the right. Both have color code B14 and appear to be the same color.

(b) The "Dark" (Black, Brown, and Grey) Family

BLACK (D12)/1948; GUNMETAL BLACK (D21 & 12)/ 1937-38, 1939-47 (Figures 3.2-10 through 12): The color name Black represents the lush glossy black that is found on many of the pieces offered in the last three catalogs (1948 to 1950). This color name appeared in those catalogs with the description: "High luster." However, the code D12 appeared from 1939 to 1947 but was associated with the color name Gunmetal Black which had a materially different description: "A metallic black with iridescent blue metal sheen." The color name Gunmetal Black succeeded the name Bronze Black (D21) which appeared in the first three catalogs (1934-35) and Metallic Black (D21) which appeared in one catalog in 1937. The name Gunmetal Black (D21) first appeared in 1938 with the same code (D21) and same description as its two predecessors:

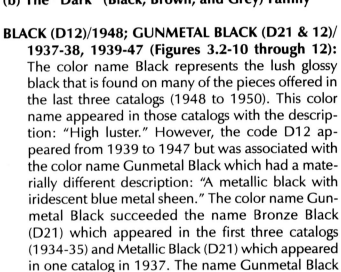

Figure 3.2-10
Gloss Black with colored interiors—Jonquil Yellow is on the right (this two-tone was part of the Standard palette for 1950).

148

"A metallic black matt with iridescent blue steel sheen." In 1939, Gunmetal Black changed codes to D12 but kept the same description until 1947 when it appeared for the last time with the misbegotten description: "High luster." Black gloss is shown in Figure 3.2-10 with Jonquil Yellow and blue interiors. Figure 3.2-11 shows a Gunmetal Black Swedish vase.

Figure 3.2-11
Gunmetal Black Swedish vase (314). *Courtesy of Knoxville Museum.*

Figure 3.2-12
Hybrid black color with elements of metallic sheen and high gloss.

COPENHAGEN GRAY (D13)/1940-41; GREY (D13)/ 1950 (Figure 3.2-13): The color name Copenhagen Gray appeared in the Fall of 1940 and again in the Spring of 1941 with the description: "A new color creation for the present day color trend. A neutral gloss color like the famous Gray of Copenhagen." The color code D13 appeared again in 1950 but with the color name of Grey and the description: "A lovely pastel blue-grey." These are two different colors, one being a glossy "battleship" type grey and the other a less glossy bluish pastel.

Figure 3.2-13
Two grey colors. The left is the pastel "Grey" issued in 1950. The right is the Copenhagen Gray issued in 1940. Note the "clear coat" look to the vase on the right which is characteristic of Copenhagen Grey.

COPPER BROWN (D23)/1935-36 (Figures 3.14 and 15): This is the only brown color listed in the catalogs, although several shades of brown do exist. All browns are sought by collectors. This color is listed in catalogs of Spring of 1935 through Spring 1936 with the description: "A warm semi-matt metallic copper brown with iridescent sheen. A mottled glaze with a charm that will last." This color has black specks the size of coarse ground pepper. Some browns are iridescent and some are not. Those of iridescent hue are remarkable.

Figure 3.2-14
Examples of Copper Brown—Early Pieces designed by Eric Hertslet. *Courtesy of Christine and Jamie Boone.*

Figure 3.2-15
A later piece in a lighter shade of brown.

(c) The Green Family

APRIL GREEN (G15)/1939-40 (Figure 3.2-16): This color appeared in four catalogs (1939 to 1940) with the following description: "A lustrous yellow-green glaze of proven popularity."

Figure 3.2-16
April Green Small Egret vase (487)/14H/1939-50.

Figure 3.2-17
Celedon Green window box (570D)/10L/
1942-46

Figure 3.2-18
Fern Green *Classic*
vase 174.

CELEDON GREEN (G25 and G11)/1936-47 (Figure 3.2-17): This color first appeared in the Fall of 1936 coded as G25 with the color name Celedon and the description: "A gloss glaze like the old Chinese celedon." In the next four catalogs (1937 through 1938) the code was the same but the description was slightly different: "A glossy grayed-green like the old Chinese celedon." The color called Celedon Green appeared in two more catalogs, (1942 and 1947) but with the code G11 and with another slightly different description: "A cool grayed-green like the old Chinese celedon." There are many slight variations of this color.

FERN GREEN (G16)/1941 (Figure 3.2-18): Appeared in the two catalogs for 1941 with the description: "A medium green of deep forest coloring."

LAKE GREEN (G23)/1935 (Figure 3.2-19): This color appeared in only the Fall 1934 Catalog with the description: "A mottled light green, semi-matt texture."

Figure 3.2-19
Lake Green, one with more brown
dappling than the other. *Courtesy of
Robert Rush.*

REGENCY GREEN (G24)/1935-36 (Figure 3.2-20) This color appeared in 1935 and 1936 with the description: "A deep blue-green matt. Ideal for the modern interior and perfect for flower containers."

Figure 3.2-20
Regency Green 351/Vase/Capri/5.75H/
1935-37 with Fire Red 312/Vase/Han/6H/
1934-49; Copper Brown (non-iridescent
)/309/Vase/Neo-Classic (Bell Crater Urn)/
12.5H/1034-36; and Royal Blue 343/
Plate/Coupe Service/12D/1935. *Courtesy
of Robert Rush.*

SILVER GREEN (G14)/1938-40 (Figure 3.2-21): This color appeared in Spring of 1938 to the Fall of 1940 with the description: "a soft gray-green matt." This color was offered on *LaFleur* and *Classic* artware only.

SPRUCE (G17)/1948-50 (Figure 3.2-22): This color appeared in the last three catalogs (1948, 1949, and 1950) with the description: "A light luster different shade of green."

ROYAL CHARTREUSE (C10)/1949-50 (Figure3.2-22): Listed as "A delicate Abingdon shade."

Figure 3.2-21
Silver Green Gamma *Classic* vase (107)/
8H/1938-39.

Figure 3.2-22
Spruce, Ming white, Sierra, and Royale
Chartreuse.

(d) The Red Family

AUTUMN PEACH (T20); PEACH (T20 & R12)/1937-38 (Figure 3.2-23): The color name Autumn Peach (T20) appeared in only one catalog (Fall 1937) with the following description: "A delightful new color in harmony or pleasing contrast with any other color. A new ceramic color developed by Abingdon." Peach (T20 and R12) first appeared in the Fall of 1937 with the code T20; it next appeared in the Spring 1938 catalog with the code R12; and, it finally appeared in the Fall of 1938 with the code T20 again. No description at all was provided in the Fall of 1938 but the same description in the Fall of 1937 and the Spring of 1938: "A warm peach coloring in mottled glossy glaze."

CAMEO (R19)/1948-50 (Figure 3.2-24): This color was offered in the last three catalogs (1948-50) as: "a light pink shade in pastel." This is one of three red color names with the word "Cameo" in it. The other two have identical names (Cameo Pink) but do have different color codes and descriptions.

CAMEO PINK (R17)/1941; CAMEO PINK (R18)/1942-47 (Figure 3.2-25): Cameo Pink with the color code R17 was offered in 1941 as: "A medium shade of pink or dusty coral." Cameo Pink with the color code R18 was offered in 1942 through 1947 with the description: "A light pink shade in a soft waxy matt texture." The 1942 catalog offered the Starflower Collection in Celedon Green, Cameo Pink (R18), and Cool Blue shown in 3.2-25. R17 can not be isolated for illustration.

Figure 3.2-23
Autumn Peach
3906/Sculpture/
Shephardess and
Fawn/11.5H/
1937-38. *Courtesy of Knoxville Museum.*

Figure 3.2-24
Cameo 638/Calla
vase/8.5H/1948.
Courtesy of Christine and Jamie Boone.

Figure 3.2-25
Cameo Pink Starflower cache pot (559D/5.5H/1942) with Cool Blue low cornucopia (569/8L/1947-48) and Celedon Green window box (570D/10L/1947-50).

DUBONNET (R13 and R21); ROYAL RED (R21)/1934-47 (Figures 3.2-26): Dubonnet first appeared with the name Royal Red and color code of R21 in the Fall of 1934 with the following description: "A purplish red in a semi-gloss glaze." The description changed over the next three years to: "A rich red of slight bluish tint with great depth of color." In the Spring of 1938, the name Royal Red was replaced with the name Dubonnet, with no change in color code or description. To confuse things completely, in this same catalog (Spring 1938), Dubonnet appeared with another color code (R13) but no description at all. Thus, Dubonnet was found with two color codes in one catalog. It should be noted that the Dubonnet with the code R13 was offered on one piece only in the Spring 1938 catalog, the refrigerator water jug that was offered only in this particular catalog. One way to isolate this color would be to find a water jug in dark red. Two years later the color name Dubonnet was paired for keeps with the color code R13 with the following description: "The ever popular decorative color as only Abingdon can produce." No indication here of an actual color change to accompany the code change. In Figure 3.2-26, Little Dutch Girl is in Sudan Red next to a Rosette vase and a Fairfield vase in Royal Red. Sudan Red could be mistaken by the untrained eye for Royal Red.

FAWN (R16)/1941 (Figure 3.2-27 and 28): This color appeared in 1941 with the description: "A light tan with a warm pinkish tint—beige." It can be confused with Blonde but Fawn is darker with more red.

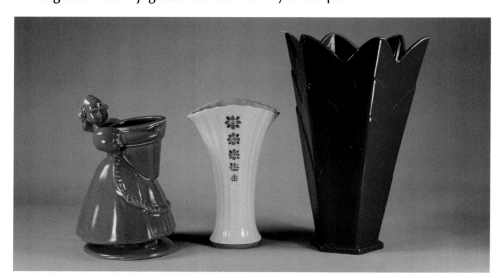

Figure 3.2-26

Figure 3.2-27
Fawn Squatty vase (552/8.5D/1941-48) with Dolphin bookends/vases (444/5.75H/1938-49). Compare with Blonde Fruit Girl (3904) in Figure 3.2-28. Fawn and Blonde are similar but Fawn has a little more red.

Figure 3.2-28
Blonde Fruit Girl (3904) 1935-37/10H. Lighter than Fawn.

FIRE RED (R31)/1934-35 (Figures 3.2-29 and 30): This color appeared in the first two catalogs (Fall of 1934 and Spring of 1935) only. In the Fall 1934 catalog it was described as: "A brilliant glaze with a crystalline sparkle." In the Spring 1935 catalog it was described as: "A brilliant, red orange with a crystalline sparkle. A color that will warm up that dark corner." The Fall 1935 catalog announced that this color had been discontinued. This is a beautiful color and extremely rare. The Double Cornucopia (#482) was not in-troduced in the catalogs until 1939, several years after Fire Red (R31) was supposed to have been discontinued. Note that there is a slight difference in color when comparing the two figures.

PEACH GLOW (R14)/1940 (Figure 3.2-31): This color appeared in 1940 with the description: "A deep shade of pink or dusty coral." Similar in name to Autumn Peach(T20)/Peach (T20 & R12) and Peach Bloom Pink (R11).

Figure 3.2-29 Original Fire Red 313/Bowl/Rope/ 10.5D/1934-36 with 323/ Candleholders/ 3.75D/1934-36 and 324/Vases/ Rope/6H/1934-38, 1947-48. Compare to Double Cornucopia in 3.2-30 which is slightly different in color.

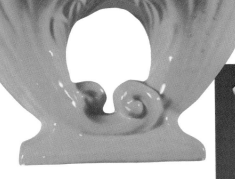

Figure 3.2-30
A piece not offered until 1939 in a color similar to Fire Red, a color officially discontinued in 1935. The piece is 482/ Double Cornucopia/11L/1939-50. *Courtesy of Knoxville Museum.*

Figure 3.2-31
Large and Small Acanthus (486/14H/ 1939-50 and 485/11H/1939-40) with small vase in Peach Glow.

PEACH BLOOM PINK (R11)/1935-37 (Figure 3.2-32): This color appeared in 1935-37. It was described as: "A pleasing pink gloss textured glaze…" Two other colors listed below have similar sounding names, Autumn Peach (T20)/Peach (T20 and R12) and Peach Glow (R14). They both have codes and descriptions different from Peach Bloom Pink.

SUDAN RED (T10)/1939-40 (Figure 3.2-33): This color appears from 1939 to 1940 with the description: "A warm reddish tan of semi-matt texture." This is a medium to dark red but much less impressive than the darker, richer Royal Red/Dubonnet.

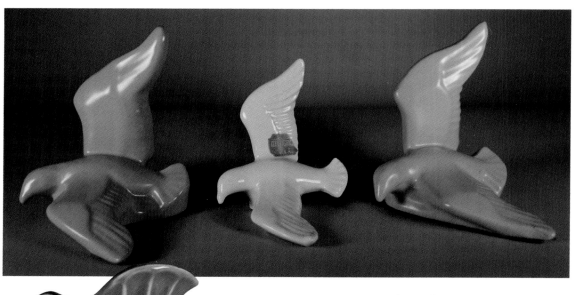

Figure 3.2-32
Peach Bloom Pink
305/Bookends/
Seagull/6H/1934-
42 with 562/
Animal Figure/
Gull/5H/1942.

Figure 3.2-33
Sudan Red 200/
Jug/Ice Lipped
Pitcher/2 Quart/
1940-41.

(e) The White Family

ANTIQUE WHITE (W21 and W14)/1934-47 (Figure 3.2-34): The color name Antique White appeared in 15 catalogs, from 1934 to 1947. The color code W21 was used until 1939 when it was replaced by W14. The descriptions for each code were only slightly different. Code W21 read: "A beautiful off-white glaze with soapstone texture." Code W14 read: "An off-white matt with smooth waxen surface." Note: The color name White (W14) appeared in 1938 but with no description other than to say that the color White was offered on *LaFleur* and *Classic* pieces only.

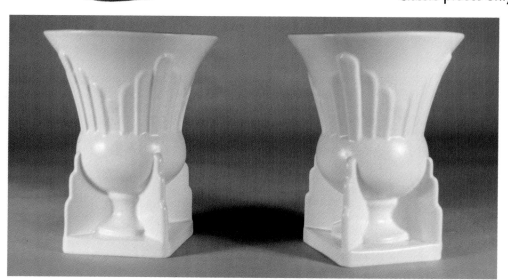

Figure 3.2-34
Antique White 351/Vase/Capri/5.75/
1935-37.

BLONDE (W23)/1936-38 (Figure 3.2-35): This color appeared in five catalogs (1936 through 1938) with the description: "A semi-gloss glaze in the color like that of the popular blonde woods" in the first three catalogs and in the last two catalogs it was described as: "a bright glaze of warm ivory coloring." Similar to but lighter than Fawn.

EGGSHELL (W16 & W17)/1939-47 (Figure 3.2-36): This color appeared from 1939 to 1947 with the description: "A high luster glaze with a delicate ivory coloring." However, in the first two catalogs (1939), the color code was W16 but in the others, W17.

MING WHITE (W26)/1948-50 (Figure 3.2-37): This color appeared in the last three catalogs (1948 through 1950) with the description: "An ivory white with a beautiful sheen." A color called Ivory (W15) appeared in the Fall of 1938 and was offered on the refrigerator water jug (mold #113). No description was provided. NOTE: nearly all hand-painted pieces used ivory colored backgrounds.

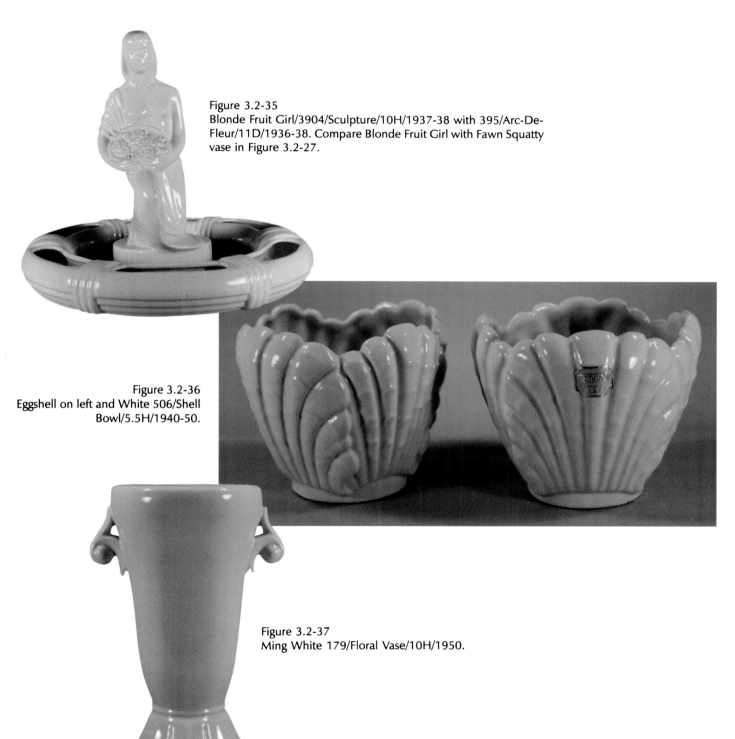

Figure 3.2-35
Blonde Fruit Girl/3904/Sculpture/10H/1937-38 with 395/Arc-De-Fleur/11D/1936-38. Compare Blonde Fruit Girl with Fawn Squatty vase in Figure 3.2-27.

Figure 3.2-36
Eggshell on left and White 506/Shell Bowl/5.5H/1940-50.

Figure 3.2-37
Ming White 179/Floral Vase/10H/1950.

(f) The Yellow Family

GOLDEN YELLOW (Y11)/1939-40 (Figure 3.2-38): This color appeared in four catalogs (1939-40) with the description: "The name describes this gloss glaze." It was offered on the *Classic* line, on the garden and solarium vases, floor vases, and sand jars.

JASMINE YELLOW (Y13)1939-40 (Figure 3.2-39): This color appeared in four catalogs (1939-40) with the description: "A gloss yellow with slight greenish tint (chartreuse)."

JONQUIL YELLOW (Y15)/1941-47 (Figure 3.2-40): This color appeared in four catalogs (1941 through 1947) with the description: "A transparent, high luster basic yellow."

LEMON YELLOW (Y21)/1934 (Figure 3.2-41): This color appeared in only the first catalog (Fall 1934) with the description: "A brilliant gloss glaze."

YELLOW CHARTREUSE; YELLOW (Y22)/1935-38 (Figure 3.2-42): The color Yellow Chartreuse appeared in catalogs in 1935-36 with the code Y22 and the description: "A brilliant yellow with chartreuse tint." The color with the name "Yellow" appeared in 1938 with the same code and description.

Figure 3.2-38
Golden Yellow
200/Jug/Ice
Lipped Pitcher/2
Quart/1940-41.

Figure 3.2-39
Jasmine Yellow
499/Vase/
Bookend/Trojan
Head/7.5H/1940-
41.

Figure 3.2-40
Jonquil Yellow 599/Quilted Vase/9H/1947-50. This is the Two-Tone Black offered in the 1950 palette with Gloss Black outside and Jonquil Yellow inside.

Figure 3.2-41
Lemon Yellow
302/Vase/Lung/
11H/1934-38.

Figure 3.2-42
Yellow Chartreuse is one of four 344/Wild Rose Plates/10 x 12/ 1935-36 (others in Antique White, Dawn Blue, and Peach Bloom Pink) and one Apple Blossom Plate 415/11.5D/1937 which was offered in the catalog in Dawn Blue only. Note that this is a different blue than the Dawn Blue of the Wild Rose plate. No explanation for this discrepancy. *Courtesy of Robert Rush.*

UNCATALOGED COLORS

Several colors have been documented that were not presented in the catalogs. All are very rare. The mottled ivory and blue in Figure 3.2-43 is an example. The color in Figure 3.2-44 is lavender, found on many pre-artware era pieces. The two-tone Royale Chartreuse over Ivory

in Figure 3.2-45 is atypical in that it is a two-tone with soft blending of the colors. The mottled green on the pre-artware era Egyptian vase in Figure 3.2-46 came in various degrees of mottling. The "weathered green" Russian bookends in Figure 3.2-47 are considered one of a kind. The mother-of-pearl Scroll bowl in Figure 3.2-48 is a truly stunning piece.

Figure 3.2-43
Mottled blue over ivory—uncatalogued color on 301/Jar/Ming/7.25H/1934-36.

Figure 3.2-44
Lavender—uncataloged color.

Figure 3.2-45
Royale Chartreuse accent over ivory—uncataloged combination on 181/Vase/10H/1950.

Figure 3.2-46
Mottled green—uncataloged color on 861/Egyptian vase.

Figure 3.2-47
Weathered green—uncataloged on 321/Bookends/Russian/6.5H/1934-40.

Figure 3.2-48
Mother-of-pearl with gold trim—uncataloged color on 480/Bowl/Scroll/14.5L/1939-50.

This chapter divides decorations into two groups: those pieces decorated by Abingdon Pottery staff and those pieces decorated by outside decorating firms, i.e., decorating firms that bought blank pieces of Abingdon Pottery artware, decorated that artware using their own designs and tastes, and then sold them to the public.

4.1 ABINGDON DECORATIONS

The first decorated piece offered by Abingdon appeared on the cover of the first catalog which was issued in the Fall of 1934. That piece, Neo-Classic vase or the Grecian Bell Crater Urn (309), is shown in Figures 4.1-1a and b. No other decorated pieces appeared in any of the catalogs until the Spring of 1942, more than six years later.

In the Spring of 1942, two cookie jars (Little Ol' Lady and Hippo) were first offered in three different decorations—termed, simply enough, Decorations A, B, and C. Figure 4.1-2 is a catalog reprint of the first appearance of these decorated pieces; modern photos of these pieces are found in Figures 4.1-2a through d.

Not only were these two cookie jars offered in hand-painted versions in 1942, so were 10 new pieces introduced for the first time in this Spring 1942 catalog. Figure 4.1-3 is a catalog reprint of these 10 new pieces which were first offered with white starflowers painted over three body colors: Cool Blue, Celedon Green, and Cameo Pink. Modern photos of these pieces are displayed in the 4.1-3 series of figures. This group was never given a name in the catalogs but will be referred to in this book as "The Starflower Collection." These pieces were the only group with colored bodies and white painting (nearly all other hand-painted pieces turned out to be colored painting on white bodies). Yet, in rare instances, Starflower pieces with white bodies and colored glazes were produced. In addition, the Starflower pieces without painting were produced in these three colors as well as yellow.

In 1947, Abingdon became very aggressive in offering hand-painted pieces of all kinds and remained so until the closing of the Artware Division three years later. The 4.1-4 series of figures is a composite of the color catalog pages offering hand-painted pieces from 1947 to 1950.

Figure 4.0-1a, b, and c.
497D/Vase/Blackamoor/7.5H/1940 This sequence of photos demonstrates the amount of detail and quality on Abingdon hand-painted pieces. *Courtesy of Elaine Westover.*

Figure 4.1-1a
Neo-Classic Bell Crater Urn (309/12.5H/1934-36). First decorated piece offered by Abingdon. *Courtesy of Robert Rush.*

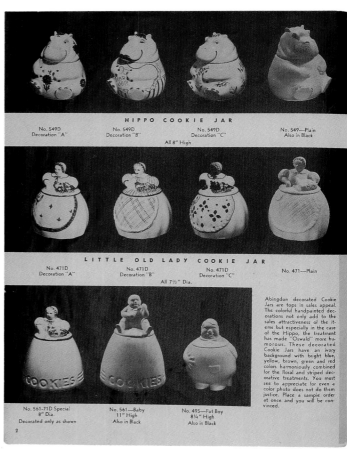

Figure 4.1-2a
Spring 1942 catalog page reprint that first introduced hand-painted cookie jars.

Figure 4.1-1b
Copper Brown version of Neo-Classic Bell Crater Urn (309/12.5H/ 1934-36). *Courtesy of Christine and Jamie Boone.*

Figure 4.1-2b
Decorations A, B, and C respectively for Little Ol' Lady (471/7.25D/1939-46). *Courtesy of Brian and Anita Hickok.*

Figure 4.1-2c
Decoration A and C for Hippo (549/8H/7D/1941-47).

Figure 4.1-3
Starflower Collection as it debuted in Spring 1942 catalog.

Figure 4.1-2d
Decoration B for Hippo (549/8H/7D/1941-47). *Courtesy of Brian and Anita Hickok.*

Figure 4.1-3a
White body with blue paint—atypical for the Starflower Collection. Coolie Jar (308D/11H/1942-46).

Figure 4.1-3b
Three pieces from the Starflower Collection: Cool Blue cache pot MD (559D/5.5H/1942); Celedon Green window box (570D/10L/1942-46); and Cameo Pink Scallop vase (566D/9H/1942-46).

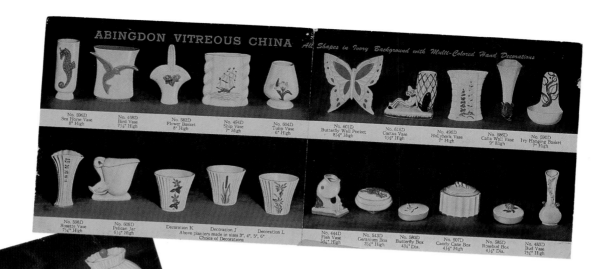

All Shapes in Ivory Background with Multi-Colored Hand Decorations

No. 596D
Sea Horse Vase
8" High

No. 468D
Bird Vase
7½" High

No. 582D
Flower Basket
8" High

No. 454D
Ship Vase
7" High

No. 604D
Tulip Vase
6" High

No. 601D
Butterfly Wall Pocket
8¼" High

No. 616D
Cactus Vase
6½" High

No. 496D
Hollyhock Vase
7" High

No. 586D
Calla Wall Vase
9" High

No. 590D
Ivy Hanging Basket
7" High

No. 598D
Rosette Vase
7¼" High

No. 609D
Pelican Jar
6½" High

Decoration K

Decoration J

Decoration L

Above planters made in sizes 3", 4", 5", 6"
Choice of Decorations

No. 444D
Fish Vase
5¼" High

No. 543D
Geranium Box
3¼" High

No. 580D
Butterfly Box
4¾" Dia.

No. 607D
Candy Cane Box
4¾" Dia.

No. 585D
Rosebud Box
4¾" Dia.

No. 483D
Bud Vase
7½" High

No. 602D
Hobby Horse Cookie Jar
10½" High

No. 549D
Hippo Cookie Jar
8" High

No. 695D
Kangaroo
7" High

No. 588D
Money Bag Cookie Jar
7½" High

No. 471D
Grandma Cookie Jar
9" High

No. 574D
Heron
5½" High

No. 372D
Pelican
5½" High

No. 571D
Goose
9" High

No. 573D
Penguin
5" High

No. 611D
Jack-in-the-Box Cookie Jar
11" High

Figure 4.1-4
A composite of catalog pages dealing with
hand-painted pieces.

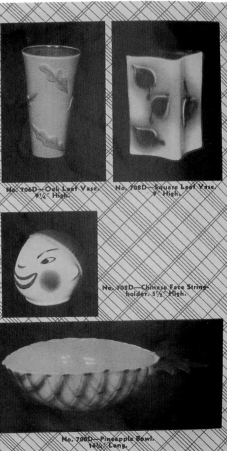

PRACTICAL ★ ABINGDON ★ CREATIONS

No. 675D—Match Box Wall Vase.
5½" High.

No. 699D—Apron Wall Vase.
6" High.

No. 712D—Mouse Stringholder.
8½" High.

No. 706D—Oak Leaf Vase.
9¼" High.

No. 708D—Square Leaf Vase.
9" High.

No. 715D—Bamboo Console Plate.
10¼" Diameter.

No. 702D—Chinese Face Stringholder. 5½" High.

No. 716D—Bamboo Candleholders.
3½" Square.

No. 616D—Cactus Vase.
6½" High.

No. 700D—Pineapple Bowl.
14¼" Long.

PAGE 10

164

4.2 NON-ABINGDON DECORATIONS

There are two types of non-Abingdon decoration: hand-painted decoration and decal decoration. Decal decorations are the most common. Hand-painted decorations are much more rare and many are not above the ordinary. However, some hand-painted decoration is extremely good. Figures 4.2-1 through 7 present hand-painted pieces done by outside firms or individual artists. Note the outside company mark in Figure 4.2-5 as the decoration on pieces with this particular mark are usually of high quality. Two silver overlay pieces are shown in Figures 4.2-8 and 9. The remaining pieces are decal-decorated pieces, and/or those with gold decoration. Some purists feel non-Abingdon decoration clashes with Abingdon's original designs.

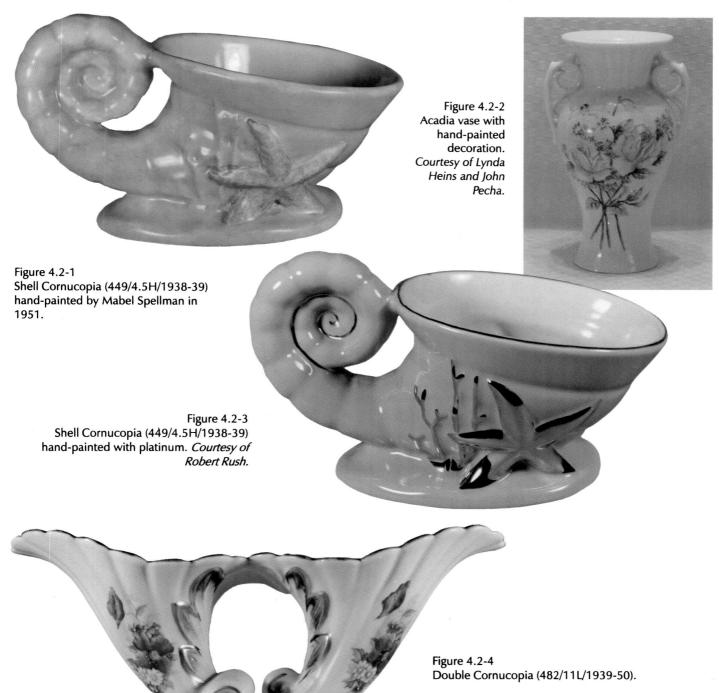

Figure 4.2-2
Acadia vase with hand-painted decoration. *Courtesy of Lynda Heins and John Pecha.*

Figure 4.2-1
Shell Cornucopia (449/4.5H/1938-39) hand-painted by Mabel Spellman in 1951.

Figure 4.2-3
Shell Cornucopia (449/4.5H/1938-39) hand-painted with platinum. *Courtesy of Robert Rush.*

Figure 4.2-4
Double Cornucopia (482/11L/1939-50).

Figure 4.2-5
Bottom of Double
Cornucopia
shown in previous
illustration.
Decoration on
pieces with this
mark are most
often of very good
quality.

Figure 4.2-6
Oval Shell vase (507/7.5H/1940).

Figure 4.2-7
Swirl vase (513/9H/1940-50).

Figure 4.2-8
Classic vase (116/
10H/1939-1949)
with Sterling silver
overlay. *Courtesy
of Brian and Anita
Hickok.*

Figure 4.2-9
Acanthus vase
(486/11H/1939-
1950) with
Sterling silver
overlay. *Courtesy
of Betty Perry.
Photo taken by
Tom Foley of
Midwest Photo.*

Figure 4.2-10 Draped vases (557/11H/1941-48) with decals and gold trim.

Figure 4.2-11 Abbey vase (515/7H/1940-50) with decals and gold trim.

Figure 4.2-12 Two Baden vases (520/9H/1940-48) with decals and gold trim.

Figure 4.2-13
More Baden vases (520/9H/1940-48) with decals and trim.

Figure 4.2-14.
Boyne vase (534/9H/1941-46) with decals and gold trim. *Courtesy of Brian and Anita Hickok.*

167

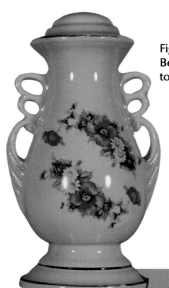

Figure 4.2-15
Berne vase (535/9H/1941-46) converted to lamp base with decal and gold trim.

Figure 4.2-16
Scroll double candlesticks (479/4.5H/1939-50).

Photo 4.2-17
Barre vase (522/9H/1940-50) with decals and gold trim.

Figure 4.2-19
Scroll bowl MD (532/14.5L/1941-50) and Scroll double candlesticks (479/4.5H/1939-50) with decals and gold trim—common decoration.

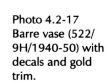

Figure 4.2-18
Fluted vase (550/11H/1941-50) with decals and gold trim.

Figure 4.2-20
Scroll bowl MD (532/14.5L/1941-50) and Scroll double candlesticks (479/4.5H/1939-50) with decals and gold trim—unusual and sought after decoration.

Figure 4.2-21
Scallop bowl (564/11L/1942-50) and Scallop double candleholders (575/5H/1942-50) with decals and gold trim.

Figure 4.2-22
Round bulb bowl (518/12D/1940-50) with decals and gold trim. *Courtesy of Betty Perry. Photo taken by Tom Foley of Midwest Photo.*

Figure 4.2-23
Two Shell double candleholders (505/4H/1940-49) and one Shell console bowl LG (500/15L/1940-49).

Figure 4.2-25
Little Dutch Boy (469/8H/1939-40) and Little Dutch Girl (470/8H/1939-40). *Courtesy of Christine and Jamie Boone.*

Figure 4.2-26a
Barre vase (522/9H/1940-50).

Figure 4.2-27
Mantlepiece made from Grecian Urn (553/13H/1941-46). *Courtesy of Christine and Jamie Boone.*

Figure 4.2-29
Two rare mantlepieces. *Courtesy of Lynda Heins and John Pecha.*

Figure 4.2-26
Alpha *Classic* vase (101/10H/1938-49). *Courtesy of Christine and Jamie Boone.*

Figure 4.2-28
Mantlepiece made from Baden vase (520/9H/1940-48).

5.1 OVERVIEW

A total of 23 different cookie jar body shapes were advertised in the catalogs. A 24th body shape, Abingdon Mammy (see Figures 5.1-1a and b), was made in a quantity of 20 to 25. According to Abingdon Pottery Collector's Club Historian, Robert Rush, these jars were made for the distributors in Chicago, Illinois, as a reward for their outstanding efforts in marketing Abingdon pottery.

Figure 5.1-1a
Abingdon Mammy
22H with Humpty
Dumpty 663/
10.5H/1949-50.
*Courtesy of Kathy
Cleer.*

Figure 5.1-1b
Abingdon Mammy
22H rear view.
*Courtesy of Kathy
Cleer.*

The first four cookie jars (Little Ol' Lady 1939; Fatboy, 1940, Hippo and Baby, 1941) were the only jars offered in single-color glazes. The first hand-painted cookie jars (Little Ol' Lady and Hippo) were offered in 1942. All cookie jars were eventually offered in hand-painted varieties, even the first four which were offered in single-colors only until 1942. Single-color cookie jars last appeared in the Spring 1942 catalog. Note, however, that this catalog was reprinted until 1947. All hand-painted jars except Pineapple, Pumpkin, and the bottom of Humpty Dumpty, have ivory colored bodies over which colors were painted.

The years in which each of the 23 production model cookie jars were introduced in the catalogs are:

1939 Little Ol' Lady (471)
1940 Fatboy (495)
1941 Baby (561); Hippo (549)
1942 Special 561-71
1947 Hobby Horse (602); Jack-in-the-Box (611); Money Bag (588)
1948 Choo Choo (602); Clock (653)
1949 Daisy (677); Humpty Dumpty (663); Miss Muffet (662); Pineapple (664); Pumpkin (674); Wigwam (665); Windmill (678)
1950 Bo Peep (694); Floral/Plaid (697); Little Girl (693); Mother Goose (695); Three Bears (696); Witch (692)

Three jars (Little Ol' Lady, Hippo, and Floral/Plaid) were made in more than one decoration scheme. Abingdon decorators were allowed to improvise and, thus, variations exist of the "official" decoration schemes displayed in the catalogs.

Two jars (Choo Choo and Clock) have one decoration scheme but with more than one set of colors within that scheme. Both were first offered in 1948, the only new jars offered that year.

As Mr. Lewis's manuscript pointed out, molds were sold by Abingdon to Pidgeon Vitreous China Company, Barnhart, Missouri, in 1950 when the Artware Division closed. Pidgeon did make cookie jars from 1950 until they went out of business in 1953 and cookie jars have been found that are identical to Abingdon with the Pidgeon sticker on them.

Regal China Company, Antioch, Illinois, also made jars nearly identical to Abingdon. Regal is known to have made the following jars: Miss Muffet, Hobby Horse, and Humpty Dumpty (see Figures 5.1-2a, b, and c). The mold numbers of Regal are different from Abingdon's: Regal's Miss Muffet is 705 vs. Abingdon's 662; Hobby Horse is 706 vs. 602; Humpty Dumpty is 707 vs. 663. Regal's Humpty Dumpty is accompanied by the words "Humpty Dumpty" impressed on the bottom above the mold number.

Figure 5.1-2d shows a poor reproduction (not Regal or Pidgeon) next to a genuine Abingdon. However, look carefully at Figure 5.1-2e showing two Little Ol' Lady cookie jars. The jar on the right has the Abingdon stamp but is cold painted and the glaze is said to be different than the glaze on the left. Is it Abingdon? Former employees consistently say that Abingdon never did any cold painting. How then can the Abingdon stamp be explained on a cold painted piece? It can't. Either Abingdon did cold painting and memories have failed or Abingdon did not and the piece in the photo is not Abingdon—or at least it was not decorated by Abingdon.

Figure 5.1-2a
Miss Muffet: Abingdon (662) right; Regal (705) left. *Courtesy of Kathleen Maloney.*

Figure 5.1-2c
Humpty Dumpty: Abingdon (663) right; Regal (707) left. *Courtesy of Kathleen Maloney.*

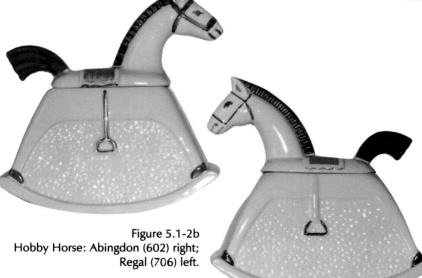

Figure 5.1-2b
Hobby Horse: Abingdon (602) right; Regal (706) left.

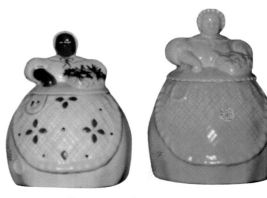

Figure 5.1-2d
Little Ol' Lady reproduction on the left; Little Ol' Lady (471/7.5D/1939-47) original on the right. Note the difference in size.

Figure 5.1-2e
Courtesy of Kathleen Maloney.

The 5.1-3 series of Illustrations show "Prototype Hippo" which was painted by Bernice McMillan, the talented painter that managed the hand-painting activities once Abingdon began offering such pieces. This decoration for Hippo was never put into production because the level of detail would not make it cost-effective to produce. It is believed that the quality and charm of the decoration helped convince Abingdon's management to offer hand-painted jars.

Figure 5.1-3
Prototype Hippo.

5.2 COOKIE JAR DICTIONARY

1. **BABY 561/11H/1941-42 (Figures 5.2-1a and b):** Introduced in 1941 with the color palette of: Frost Blue; Fern Green; Cameo Pink; Antique White; Eggshell; Jonquil Yellow; and, Gunmetal Black. Baby was offered in all seven of these colors. Baby did not appear in the catalogs issued 1947-50.
2. **BO PEEP 694/12H/1950 (Figure 5.2-2):** Only one decoration scheme of Bo Peep was made by Abingdon.

Figure 5.2-1a

Figure 5.2-1b

Figure 5.2-2
Courtesy of Brian and Anita Hickok.

3. CHOO CHOO 651/7.5H/1948-50 (Figure 5.2-3):
Abingdon made at least four color combinations for this jar: black and yellow accents; green and pink; green and bright red; light blue and pink.

4. CLOCK 653/9H/1948-50 (Figures 5.2-4a and b): In the 1948 catalog, the foot and all but the finial of the lid were white—the finial and the clock hands being a light color—probably yellow. In the 1949 catalog, the entire lid and the foot are a dark color—green, blue, and black are known to accent this jar. The picture in the 1950 catalog is the same as that for 1949.

Figure 5.2-3a
Courtesy of Brian and Anita Hickok.

Figure 5.2-3b

Figure 5.2-4a
*Courtesy of Brian
and Anita Hickok.*

Figure 5-2-4b
*Courtesy of Brian
and Anita Hickok.*

5. DAISY 677/8H/1949-50 (Figures 5.2-5a and b): Was offered with yellow flowers and also with blue flowers. Salt and pepper shakers, a grease jar, a sugar bowl, a creamer, and a tea pot were offered in the same motif and two color choices.

6. FATBOY 495/8.5H/1940-42 (Figures 5.2-6a, b, and c): Introduced in 1940 with the dimensions of 8.25 inches high and 6 inches in diameter. It was offered in the following seven colors: Ariel Blue; April Green; Peach Glow; Sudan Red; Antique White; Eggshell; Jasmine Yellow. It was offered at $18.00 per dozen. Fatboy was also offered in the following colors in the Spring of 1941: Frost Blue; Fern Green; Cameo Pink (R17); Fawn; Jonquil Yellow; Gunmetal Black. The last appearance for this jar was in the Spring of 1942 where Cool Blue and Celedon Green and Cameo Pink (R18) were introduced. While no catalog shows this cookie jar in a hand-painted variety, hand-painted varieties do exist.

Figure 5.2-6a

Figure 5.2-5a

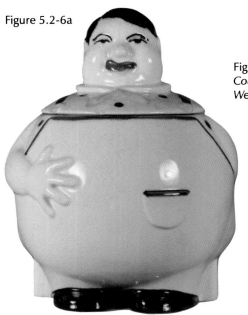

Figure 5.2-6b
Courtesy of Elaine Westover.

Figure 5.2-5b
Courtesy of Brian and Anita Hickok.

Figure 5.2-6c
Courtesy of Elaine Westover.

7. FLORAL/PLAID 697/8.5H/1950 (Figures 5.2-7a and b): Mold number 697 was listed as two different jars in the 1950 catalog. Both had the same mold number and body shape. Both are considered here as one jar with two different decoration schemes. One other Abingdon plaid design does exist and is owned by a veteran collector from Abingdon. Yet another plaid cookie jar with similar body design does exist but was not made by Abingdon.

8. HIPPO 549/8H/1941-47 (Figures 5.2-8a through d): One of the most darling of all cookie jars. Designed by Frances Moody. It was "designed at my kitchen breakfast table" as Mrs. Moody recalled in 1996—55 years after the fact. Hippo first appeared in the Fall of 1941, along with the short-lived cookie jar Baby. Both were offered in Gunmetal Black as well as: Frost Blue; Fern Green; Cameo Pink (R17); Antique White; Eggshell; Jonquil Yellow. After being introduced in the Fall 1941 catalog, Hippo appeared in the next catalog, Spring of 1942 (the catalog that was to be re-printed until 1947) in single-color decoration as well as three hand-painted varieties: Decorations A, B, and C. Hippo appeared for the last time in the hand-painted catalog for 1947. It was not present in the single-color catalog for that same year.

Figure 5.2-7a
Courtesy of Brian and Anita Hickok.

Figure 5.2-7b
Plaid in uncataloged design.

Figure 5.2-8a
Decoration A.

Figure 5.2-8b
Decoration B. *Courtesy of Brian and Anita Hickok.*

Figure 5.2-8c
Decoration C.

Figure 5.2-8d
Decoration B and
C rear view.
*Courtesy of Brian
and Anita Hickok.*

9. HOBBY HORSE 602/10.5H/1947-50 (Figure 5.2-9): Was produced by both Pidgeon Vitreous China Company of Barnhart, Missouri, and Regal China Company of Antioch, Illinois. Look for the stamp and the proper mold number. Without either, consider it suspect.

10. HUMPTY DUMPTY 663/10.5H/1949-50 (Figure 5.2-10): Abingdon's Humpty Dumpty has a yellow bottom. Red bottoms were made by Regal China Company which also made matching salt and pepper shakers. Beware, however, because Regal also made yellow bottoms. Look for the 663 and the Abingdon stamp or be suspicious. Only one Abingdon variation (yellow bottom) is shown in the catalog and no known red bottom with the Abingdon stamp has been found. NOTE: Abingdon did NOT make matching salt and pepper shakers. Regal China Company did. They are red on the bottom.

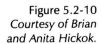

Figure 5.2-9
*Courtesy of Brian
and Anita Hickok.*

Figure 5.2-10
*Courtesy of Brian
and Anita Hickok.*

11. JACK-IN-THE-BOX 611/11H/1947-49 (Figures 5.2-11a and b): ABC is on the front and COOKIES is on the back—or vice versa, depending on what you decide is the front as it is a square and can face either way. Only one Abingdon version of Jack-in-the-Box is known.

12. LITTLE OL' LADY 471/7.5H/1939-47 (Figures 5.2-12a through d): Designed by Frances Moody who recalls that Abingdon "eventually went wild with cookie jars" after the success of the first few jars. The only cookie jar to appear in 1939, it appeared in the following seven colors: Ariel Blue; April Green;

Dubonnet; Sudan Red; Antique White; Eggshell; Jasmine Yellow; in the Spring of 1940, it was offered in another color: Peach Glow. In the Spring of 1941, it was offered in the following 6 colors not previously offered: Frost Blue; Fern Green; Cameo Pink (R17); Fawn; Jonquil Yellow; Gunmetal Black. In the Spring 1942, this jar was offered in three more colors: Cool Blue, Celedon Green; and Cameo Pink (R18). Little Ol' Lady appeared in only one more catalog: the 1947 catalog for hand-painted pieces. It did not appear in the 1947 catalog displaying only single-color pieces.

Figure 5.2-11a
Courtesy of Brian and Anita Hickok.

Figure 5.2-11b
Courtesy of Brian and Anita Hickok.

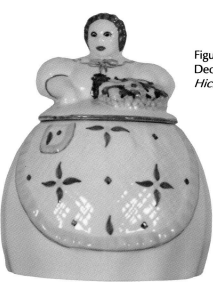

Figure 5.2-12a
Decoration A. *Courtesy of Brian and Anita Hickok.*

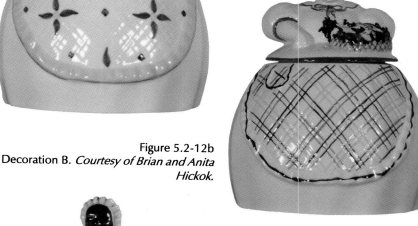

Figure 5.2-12b
Decoration B. *Courtesy of Brian and Anita Hickok.*

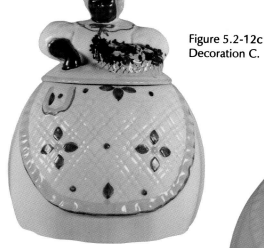

Figure 5.2-12c
Decoration C.

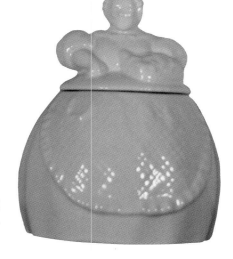

Figure 5.2-12d
Courtesy of Brian and Anita Hickok.

13. **LITTLE GIRL 693/9.5H/1950 (Figure 5.2-13):** There are look-alikes that are hard to distinguish while others are so different as to be readily recognizable as not the Abingdon original.

14. **MISS MUFFET 662/11H/1949-50 (Figure 5.2-14):** Both Pidgeon Vitreous China Company and Regal China Company made this jar. Abingdon's top has detailing on the sleeves and dress of Miss Muffet that Pidgeon does not have and that is more elaborate than the detailing on the Regal jar. In addition, the Abingdon jar has accent marks on the bottom of the jar that run in parallel and on a gentle angle from top left to bottom right. The Regal jar has accent marks slanting in both directions forming *X*s instead of parallel lines. Only one Abingdon version of this jar was made.

15. **MONEY BAG 588/7H/1947-50 (Figure 5.2-15):** This cookie jar comes in several colors but only one color combination—ivory body with pink accents—is deemed by veteran collectors to be Abingdon. Mustard yellow bodies with gold accents do exist but without the Abingdon stamp. Look for wear on the accent colors. If it is worn or if it is chipped, consider it NON-Abingdon. Almost all Abingdon cookie jars have ivory bodies: Pineapple, Pumpkin, and the bottom of Humpty Dumpty are the only exceptions. Money Bag appeared in a catalog every year from 1947 to 1950.

16. **MOTHER GOOSE 695/12H/1950 (Figure 5.2-16):** A non-Abingdon look-alike was made with a round base (unlike the Abingdon oval) and colors more intense than Abingdon. Pfaltzgraff is believed to be the maker.

Figure 5.2-13
Courtesy of Brian and Anita Hickok.

Figure 5.2/15
Courtesy of Brian and Anita Hickok.

Figure 5.2/14
Courtesy of Brian and Anita Hickok.

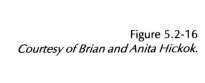

Figure 5.2-16
Courtesy of Brian and Anita Hickok.

17. PINEAPPLE 664/10.5H/1949-50 (Figure 5.2-17): One of only two (two and one half if you consider the solid yellow bottom of Humpty Dumpty) hand-painted jars (Pumpkin being the other) not having a clear ivory color for a background. Only one version of this jar was produced.

18. PUMPKIN 674/8H/1949-50 (Figure 5.2-18): One (yellow-striped) version known to exist with another (solid green) version thought to be authentic by some while disputed by others.

19. SPECIAL 561-71/8D/1942 (Figure 5.2-19): A most curious and short-lived cookie jar. It appeared in only one catalog, the Spring of 1942. The bottom of Baby (561) and a hand-painted top of Little Ol' Lady (471) went to make up Special. Special was the fifth offering of Abingdon and the last pre-WWII design. No new cookie jars were offered until 1947 when three new cookie jars appeared: Money Bag, Hobby Horse, and Jack-in-the-Box. Special is extremely rare.

20. THREE BEARS 696/8.75H/1950 (Figure 5.2-20): Regal China Company made a cookie jar similar to this one but with gold tracing accents on the figures of the three bears. The mold number for the Regal is 704 and for Abingdon is 696. Only one version was made by Abingdon.

Figure 5.2-19

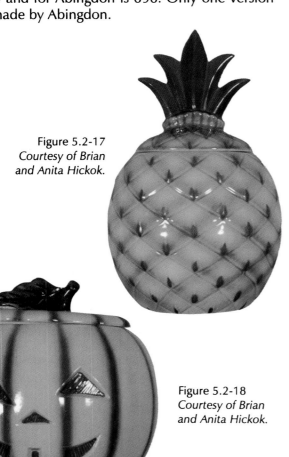

Figure 5.2-17
Courtesy of Brian and Anita Hickok.

Figure 5.2-18
Courtesy of Brian and Anita Hickok.

Figure 5.2-20

21. **WIGWAM 665/11H/1949 (Figure 5.2-21):** Sometimes referred to as Tee Pee, this jar appeared in the 1949 catalog only and only one version is known to exist.

22. **WINDMILL 678/10.5/1949 (Figure 5.2-22):** Appeared in the 1949 catalog only and only one version is known to exist.

23. **WITCH 692/11.5H/1950 (Figure 5.2-23):** Only one version made by Abingdon. No other companies known to make this jar.

Figure 5.2-21
Courtesy of Brian and Anita Hickok.

Figure 5.2-22
Courtesy of Brian and Anita Hickok.

Figure 5.2-23
Courtesy of Brian and Anita Hickok.

6. THE CATALOG REPRINTS

From the Fall of 1935 to the Fall of 1950, the Abingdon Pottery issued more than 20 catalogs. These documents totalled more than 190 pages and represent the single largest source of information about the artware. Catalog number 35 which was first issued in the Spring of 1942 was reprinted all through WWII. Catalog number 36 did not appear until Spring 1947. In 1947 and 1948, two catalogs were issued but not according to the Spring/Fall paradigm formerly used. One catalog offered only solid-color pieces and the other, a four-page color catalog, offered only hand-painted pieces. For 1949 and 1950 only one catalog was issued but with a four-page color insert for the hand-painted pieces.

What follows are selected reprinted pages from these catalogs.

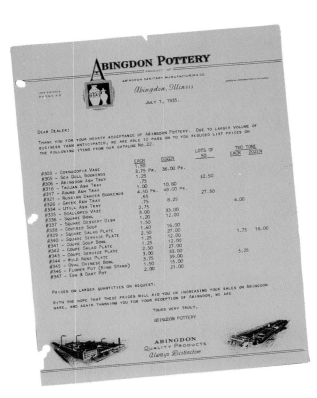

IN presenting this collection of Art Pottery it is our hope that we have been able to create a group of distinctive pieces which will find their way into the homes of those who are looking for Pottery a little better than they have been able to find at a reasonable price.

Abingdon Pottery is made of high-fired China, which means that all pieces are guaranteed to hold water and are easily identified as quality ware by the clear ring of fine China.

NEO-CLASSIC
A modern adaptation of the ancient Greek Bell Crater urn, illustrated in gold.
Neo-classic Vase No. 305
12½" high, 11x8.4 inches, $5.00

Carefully selected china clays imported from England, the finest domestic clays and Feld spar from our own mines in South Dakota, all go into the making of this fine China body.

Abingdon Pottery is well designed—there are many traditional period shapes which will long remain in style as well good period furniture. We have created pieces to fit into present day decorative schemes, whether they be modern, classic or 18th Century.

In choice of colors, we have consulted with nationally known stylists and manufacturers of fine decorative fabrics and wall coverings to make sure that our colors will blend with the smartest home furnishings.

The Abingdon Potteries have been manufacturing china for over a quarter of a century and every unit produced is of a character representing pains-taking effort to the end that the increasing demand for beauty and genuine quality in such products may be completely served.

"The clear ring of fine china"

[2]

MODERN SIMPLICITY

A DELIGHTFUL group of pieces for the dining room which, by the restrained use of a simple rope and scollop design, makes itself adaptable to almost all styles of furnishing.

The salad (or fruit) bowl is rounded on the inside for those who like to do their own mixing, and will make an admirable punch bowl for a small party.

The vases, with their Early American form, are just right for the small table bouquet.

The candle holders are designed to catch all the drippings, and candles will fit snugly without cutting or stuffing the holders with paper.

SALAD BOWL No. 313, 10½" Diameter	each $3.00
CANDLE HOLDERS No. 323, 3⅛" Diameter	pair 1.50
ROPE VASE No. 324, 6" High	each 1.00

[3]

PRACTICAL FLOWER CONTAINERS

A SQUATTY bulb bowl in the modern French manner with two large vases; the one quite frankly modern and the oval vase a pleasing Classical form.

	No.	Size	Price
FLOWER BOWL	311	7" Diam.	$1.25
FAIRFIELD VASE	307	11" high	2.50
RING VASE	318	10½" high	2.75

TWO ORIGINAL BOOK ENDS

THE Russian dancer is a delightful piece of modeling with lots of action.

The seagull is both graceful and practical.

	No.	Size	Price
RUSSIAN BOOK ENDS	321	6½" high	$4.50
SEAGULL BOOK ENDS	305	6" high	3.75

[5]

TO ADD A TOUCH OF FORMALITY

AT the top is a graceful classic vase with a simple Greek Key band around the neck. On the left a cornucopia with-out too much of the rococo usually found in this shape. On the right a decorative vase on an ivory colored stand.

	No.	Size	Price
CLASSIC VASE	315	9" high	$1.50
CORNUCOPIA	305	7½" high	pair 4.00
CALLA VASE	325	6½" high	1.50

"The clear ring of fine china"

[7]

FOR THE MODERN INTERIOR

A MODERN Swedish design in a vase and goblet which will add that sophisticated touch to the modern room. A set of three sizes in a simple flower vase with broken bands forming the decoration.

	No.	Size	Price
SWEDISH GOBLET	322	6½" high	$1.50
MODERN VASE No. 1	314	8½" high	1.75
MODERN VASE No. 2	319	7¾" high	1.25
MODERN VASE No. 3	329	6" high	1.00
	328	4½" high	.85

CHINESE CHIPPENDALE ACCESSORIES

THE two pieces in the foreground are reminiscent of fine old jade shapes of the 15th century and will enhance the modern Chinese in-terior. The vase in the background is typ-ical of the 17th Cen-tury and is mounted on a delicate stand in ebony black finish.

	No.	Size	Price
HAN VASE	312	6" high	$1.00
CHANG VASE	310	10½" high	2.25
SANG VASE	304	9½" high	1.50

[4]

184

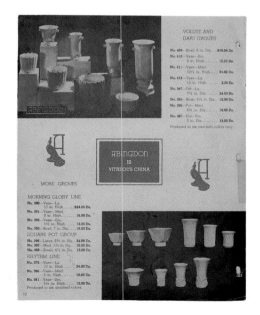

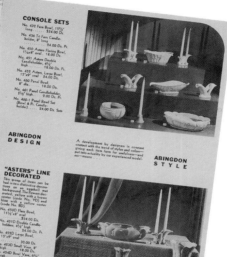

Abingdon Pottery is pleased to present for 1940 a pattern that is distinctively different—The exquisite form of the shell developed into many decorative and useful forms. Low shell bowls of three useful sizes for fruit centerpieces, sandwich plates, hors d' oeuvre, relishes (500, 501, 502). Candleholders both single and double to be used in forming your own console arrangement (503 and 505). Vases smartly styled in the shell pattern (506 and 507). A wall pocket that is an added decoration to any interior (508), and a shell planting vase that may also be used as a bookend (504). The single candleholder has the added use of an individual ash tray.

MADE IN U.S.A.
Support American Industries
BUY AMERICAN

No. 500 Large Shell Bowl, 15" Long .... $30.00 Dz.
No. 501 Medium Shell Bowl, 10½" Long .... 18.00 Dz.
No. 502 Small Shell Bowl, 7" Long .... 12.00 Dz.
No. 503 Shell Single Candleholder, Ash Tray,
    4"x3½" .... 12.00 Pr.
No. 504 Shell Planting Vase, 7½" High .... 18.00 Dz.
No. 505 Double Shell Candleholder, 4" High (Oval) 18.00 Dz. Pr.
No. 506 Shell Bowl, 6" Dia., 5½" High .... 12.00 Dz.
No. 507 Shell Vase, 7½" High (Oval) .... 12.00 Dz.
No. 508 Shell Wall Pocket, 7" High

ACANTHUS VASES

No. 485 Acanthus Vase, Small,
    8" High Oval .... $12.00 Dz.
No. 486 Acanthus Vase, Large,
    11" High Oval .... 18.00 Dz.

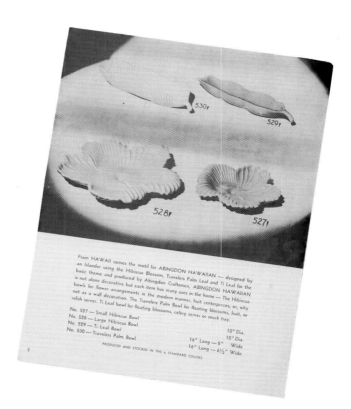

From HAWAII comes the motif for ABINGDON HAWAIIAN — designed by an Islander using the Hibiscus Blossom, Travelers Palm Leaf and Ti Leaf for the basic theme and produced by Abingdon Craftsmen, ABINGDON HAWAIIAN is not alone decorative but each item has many uses in the home — The Hibiscus bowls for flower arrangements in the modern manner, fruit centerpieces, or, why not as a wall decoration. The Travelers Palm Bowl for floating blossoms, fruit, or relish server. Ti Leaf bowl for floating blossoms, celery server or snack tray.

No. 527 — Small Hibiscus Bowl .... 10" Dia.
No. 528 — Large Hibiscus Bowl .... 15" Dia.
No. 529 — Ti Leaf Bowl .... 16" Long — 5" Wide
No. 530 — Travelers Palm Bowl .... 16" Long — 6½" Wide

PRODUCED AND STOCKED IN THE 6 STANDARD COLORS

ABINGDON presents LARGE VASES — to fill the demand for smartly styled large vases ABINGDON designers have created these new items — ABINGDON craftsmen with the most modern in manufacturing facilities have produced them in ABINGDON superior quality. The vases shown above offer an assortment of sizes and forms — both decorative and useful.

No. 550 — Fluted Vase .... 11" High
No. 552 — Squatty Vase .... 8½" Dia.
No. 553 — Grecian Urn .... 13" High
No. 554 — Ribbed Vase .... 9" High
No. 556 — Large Vase .... 12½" High
No. 557 — Draped Vase .... 11" High

PRODUCED AND STOCKED IN THE 6 STANDARD COLORS

ABINGDON.. Values Your Customers Will Appreciate

Cornucopias and Novelty Planters

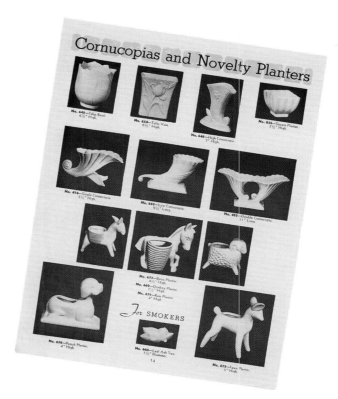

No. 642—Tulip Bowl, 6½" High
No. 654—Tulip Vase, 6½" High
No. 646—High Cornucopia, 7" High
No. 656—Square Planter, 3½" High
No. 474—Single Cornucopia, 3½" High
No. 647—Low Cornucopia, 4½" Long
No. 482—Double Cornucopia, 11" Long
No. 675—Burro Planter, 7½" High
No. 669—Donkey Planter, 7½" High
No. 671—Ram Planter, 4" High
No. 670—Pooch Planter, 4" High

For SMOKERS

No. 660—Leaf Ash Tray, 5½" Diameter
No. 679—Fawn Planter, 5" High

187

BIBLIOGRAPHY

Derwich, Jenny B. and Dr. Mary Latos. *Dictionary Guide to United States Pottery & Porcelain (19th and 20th Century)*. Jenstan, Research in United States Pottery and Porcelain, Franklin, Michigan, 1984.

Henzke, Lucile. *Art Pottery of America*. Schiffer Publishing, Ltd, Atglen, Pennsylvania, 1982.

Lewis, Albert Walter. *Abingdon, Knox County, Illinois*. The Commercial Club, Abingdon, Illinois, 1914.

Lewis, John M. Unpublished Notes and Manuscript, developed in the late 1950s and the early 1970s.

London, Rena. *Abingdon Art Pottery*. Unpublished manuscript developed in the early 1980s.

Rehl, Norma. *Abingdon Pottery*. Self-published, Milford, New Jersey, 1981.

Roerig, Joyce and Fred. *The Collector's Encyclopedia of Cookie Jars Book II*. Collector Books, Paducah, Kentucky, a Division of Schroeder Publishing Co., Inc., 1994.

Schneider, Mike. *The Complete Cookie Jar Book*. Schiffer Publishing, Ltd, Atglen, Pennsylvania, 1991.

Shoop, P. Wilbur, *Pictorial Abingdon, A Souvenir History of Abingdon, Illinois*. Published by the author, 1897.

Westfall, Ermagene. *Cookie Jars, Book II*. 1993, updated 1995.

Wright, Jesse Palmer. *Secretary Record Book*. Unpublished scrapbook kept by Mrs. Wright during the artware era, 1934-1950.

Disclaimer: This Abingdon Price Guide is not a guarantee of worth nor is it a guarantee that you will be able to buy or sell any piece of Abingdon pottery at the price listed herein. The prices herein represent my best guess on what I would have had to pay for mint condition Abingdon pottery in July of 1996—not what I should pay or want to pay.

Premium colors and non-Abingdon decorations: The prices listed in this guide do not factor in a premium paid for certain colors. Premium colors can add 25% to more than 200% to the price. No prices are provided on non-Abingdon decoration because the quality and type of decorations vary so greatly as to make pricing a case by case proposition.

N/D = Not Documented
U/C = Uncataloged

ORGANIZED BY MOLD NUMBER

MOLD#	TYPE	NAME	SIZE	YEAR	$
3801	SCULPTURE	HEAD LG	11.5H	1936-38	275
3802	SCULPTURE	HEAD SM	8.5H	1936-38	250
3901	SCULPTURE	NESCIA	16H	1935-37	UTD
3902	SCULPTURE	SCARF DANCER	13H	1935-37	325
3903	SCULPTURE	KNEELING NUDE	7H	1935-37	300
3904	SCULPTURE	FRUIT GIRL	10H	1937-38	250
03905B	CHESSMAN	BISHOP	4.5H	1937	95
03905C	CHESSMAN	CASTLE	4H	1937	95
03905K	CHESSMAN	KING	5.5H	1937	95
03905N	CHESSMAN	KNIGHT	5H	1937	95
03905P	CHESSMAN	PAWN	3.5H	1937	95
03905Q	CHESSMAN	QUEEN	5H	1937	95
3906	SCULPTURE	SHEP. & FAWN	11.5H	1937-38	225
98	ANIMAL FIGURE	GOOSE UPRIGHT	5H	1948-50	40
99	ANIMAL FIGURE	GOOSE LEANING	2.5H	1948-50	40
100	N/D				
101	VASE	ALPHA LG	10H	1938-49	20
102	VASE	BETA LG	10H	1938-39	30
103	VASE	GAMMA LG	10H	1938-39	35
104	VASE	DELTA LG	10H	1938	40
105	VASE	ALPHA MD	8H	1938-40	20
106	VASE	BETA MD	8H	1938-40	30
107	VASE	GAMMA MD	8H	1938-39	35
108	VASE	DELTA MD	8H	1938-39	40
109	VASE	ALPHA SM	6H	1938-41	20
110	VASE	BETA SM	6H	1938-41	30
111	VASE	GAMMA SM	6H	1938-39	35
112	VASE	DELTA SM	6H	1938-39	40
113	WATER JUG			1938	100
114	VASE	CLASSIC	10H	1939-46	40
115	VASE	CLASSIC	10H	1939-49	30
116	VASE	CLASSIC	10H	1939-49	30
117	VASE	CLASSIC, LG	10H	1940-49	45
118	VASE	CLASSIC, LG	10H	1940-46	35

MOLD#	TYPE	NAME	SIZE	YEAR	$
119	VASE	CLASSIC	10H	1947-49	25
120	VASE	CLASSIC	10H	1947-49	30
121-24	N/D				
125	BOWL	CLASSIC SM	11X6.5	1940-41	50
126	CANDLEHOLDER	CLASSIC, SINGLE	2X3.5	1940-41	45pr
127	BOWL	CLASSIC LG	14X6.5	1940-41	50
128-29	N/D				
130	VASE	CLASSIC, MD	8H	1940	40
131	VASE	CLASSIC, MD	8H	1940	30
132	VASE	CLASSIC, MD	8H	1940	40
133	VASE	CLASSIC, MD	8H	1940	30
134-39	N/D				
140	VASE	CLASSIC, SM	5.5H	1940-41	40
141	VASE	CLASSIC, SM	5.5H	1940-41	30
142	VASE	CLASSIC, SM	5.5H	1940-41	40
143	VASE	CLASSIC, SM	5.5H	1940-41	30
149	FLOWER POT	LA FLEUR	3H	1938-50	15
149D	FLOWER POT	LA FLEUR	3H	1938-50	25
149S	POT & SAUCER	LA FLEUR	3H	1938-50	15
150	FLOWER POT	LA FLEUR	4H	1938-46	15
150D	FLOWER POT	LA FLEUR	4H	1938-46	30
150S	POT & SAUCER	LA FLEUR	4H	1938-50	15
150	VASE	CLASSIC	9H	1941-42	25
151	FLOWER POT	LA FLEUR	5H	1947-50	15
151D	FLOWER POT	LA FLEUR	5H	1947-50	35
151S	POT & SAUCER	LA FLEUR	5H	1938-50	15
151	VASE	CLASSIC	9H	1941-42	25
152	FLOWER POT	LA FLEUR	6H	1938-50	15
152D	FLOWER POT	LA FLEUR	6H	1938-50	45
152S	POT & SAUCER	LA FLEUR	6H	1938-50	15
152	VASE	CLASSIC LG	9H	1941-46	20
153	BOWL	LA FLEUR	6D	1938-39	12
153	VASE	CLASSIC LG	9H	1941-46	40
154	VASE	CLASSIC LG	9H	1941-46	20
154	BOWL	LA FLEUR	8D	1938-39	12
155	BOWL	LA FLEUR	10D	1938-39	12
155	VASE	CLASSIC LG	9H	1941-46	25
156	BOWL	LA FLEUR	8L	1938	15
156	VASE	CLASSIC LG	9H	1942-46	15
157	BOWL	LA FLEUR	10L	1938	12
158	CANDLEHOLDER	LA FLEUR	2HX3.5D	1938-39	15
159-69	N/D				
170	VASE	CLASSIC MD	7H	1941	25
171	VASE	CLASSIC MD	7H	1941	40
172	VASE	CLASSIC MD	7H	1941	25
173	VASE	CLASSIC MD	7H	1941	40
174	VASE	CLASSIC MD	7H	1941	60
175	VASE	CLASSIC MD	7H	1941	15
176	VASE	FLORAL	10H	1950	65
177	VASE	FLORAL	10H	1950	65
178	VASE	FLORAL	10H	1950	65
179	VASE	FLORAL	10H	1950	65
180	VASE	FLORAL	10H	1950	65
181	VASE	FLORAL	10H	1950	65
182-199	N/D				
200	PITCHER	LG, ICE LIPPED	2 QT	1940-41	125
201	PITCHER	MD	1 QT	1940-41	95
202	PITCHER	SM	1 PINT	1940-41	75
252	LAMPBASE	SWIRL SHAFT	20.5H	1935	100
254	LAMPBASE	DRAPED SHAFT	21.5H	1935	100
256	LAMPBASE	SQUARE SHAFT	22.5H	1935	100
258	LAMPBASE	FLUTED SHAFT	23.5H	1935	100
301	JAR	MING	7.25H	1934-36	125
302	VASE	LUNG	11H	1934-38	225
303	CORNUCOPIA	CORNUCOPIA	7.5H	1934-36	60
304	VASE	SANG	9.5 H	1934-36	65
305	BOOKEND	SEAGULL	6 H	1934-46	150pr

MOLD#	TYPE	NAME	SIZE	YEAR	$
306	ASHTRAY	ABINGDON	8X3	1934-36	55
307	VASE	FAIRFIELD	11 H	1934-37	150
308	JAR	COOLIE	11H	1934-38	75
308D	JAR	COOLIE	11H	1942-46	100
309	VASE	NEO CLASSIC	12.5H	1934-36	125
309D	VASE	NEO CLASSIC	12.5H	1934-36	150
310	JAR	CHANG	10.5 H	1934-36	150
311	BOWL	FLOWER	6.5D	1934-36	40
312	VASE	HAN	6 H	1934-49	25
313	BOWL	SALAD BOWL	10.5 D	1934-36	75
314	VASE	SWEDISH	8.25 H	1934-36	85
315	VASE	ATHENIAN	9H	1934-36, 1947	55
316	ASHTRAY	TROJAN	5X3.5	1934-36	65
317	ASHTRAY	ROUND	5D	1934-37	25
318	VASE	RING	10.25 H	1934-37	95
319	VASE	MODERN #1	7.25 H	1934-36	90
320	VASE	TULIP	4H	1936-1937	70
321	BOOKEND	RUSSIAN	6.5 H	1934-40	300 pr
322	GOBLET	SWEDISH	6.5 H	1934-36, 1947	70
323	CANDLE HOLDER	ROPE	3.75 D	1934-36	40pr
324	VASE	ROPE	6.25H	1934-38, 47-48	35
325	VASE	CHIEN	6.5H	1934-37, 47	55
326	ASHTRAY	GREEK	4.25X3	1934-36	65
327	VASE	MODERN #2	6H	1934-36	75
328	VASE	MODERN #3	4.5 H	1934-36	75
329	STAND	FOR VASE	3.5D	1934-37	40
334	ASHTRAY	UTILITY	5.5D	1935-37	20
335	VASE	SCALLOPED	10.5L	1935-38	75
336	BOWL	SQUARE	9SQ	1935-41	60
336A	CANDLEHOLDER	HURRICANE (W/GLASS)	11H	1939-41	45pr
337	DESERT DISH	SQUARE	5SQ	1935	40
338	BOWL	SQ COVERED	4.75SQ	1935	65
339	PLATE	SQUARE SALAD	7.5SQ	1935	40
340	PLATE	SQUARE SERVICE	10.5 SQ	1935	50
341	BOWL	COUPE SOUP	5.5D	1935	45
342	PLATE	COUPE SALAD	7.5 D	1935	40
343	PLATE	COUPE SERVICE	12D	1935	55
344	PLATE	WILD ROSE	10X12	1935-36	125
345	BOWL	CHINESE OVAL	9X11	1935-37	90
346	FLOWER POT	RING STAND	5.5D	1935-36	15
347	FLOWER POT	EGG & DART	7.25D	1935-36	15
348	BOX (CIGARETTE)	TRIX	4.75X3.75	1935-37, 1947	50
349	CHALICE	CHALICE	5.5H	1935-37	100
350	VASE	FLEUR	7H	1935-38, 1947	95
351	VASE	CAPRI	5.75H	1935-37	125
352	VASE	ECHO	4H	1935-40	25
353	VASE	PENTHOUSE		1935-38	100
354	BOX	TRIXTRA	2X3	1935-37	35
355	CANDLEHOLDER	EIFEL	4.75H	1935-36	100pr
356	ASHTRAY	DUO	6.75X3.5	1936	35
357	VASE	SALON	14H	1935-38	100
358	FLOWER POT	IONIC	5H	1935-37	30
358A	FLOWER POT	IONIC LG	10.5D	1937	40
359	FLOWER POT	MART	3.5H	1935-37	20
360	CANDLEHOLDER	QUATRAIN	3SQ	1935-36	50pr
361	BOWL	TRIFORM	8X14.5	1935-37	65
362	BOWL	MONOFORM	6D	1935-36	50
363	BOOKEND	COLT	6H	1935-38	375pr
364	JAR	ELITE	4.5H	1936	50
365	JAR	DART CANDY	6.25D	1936-37	75
366	FLOWER POT	EGG & DART MD	5.25H	1936-37	20
367	FLOWER POT	EGG & DART SM	4.5H	1936-37	20
368A	CANDLEHOLDER	MODERN SM	2H	1936-38	35pr
368B	CANDLEHOLDER	MODERN MD	3H	1936-38	35pr
368C	CANDLEHOLDER	MODERN LG	4H	1936-38	35pr
369	ASHTRAY	GUARD	5SQ	1936	35
370	BOOKEND	CACTUS	6H	1936-38	100pr
371	ASHTRAY	PETITE	4D	1936-37	25
372	VASE	RHYTHM	10H	1936-37	55
373	VASE	MANHATTAN	12.5H	1936-37	115
374	BOOKEND	CACTUS PLANTER	7H	1936-38	125
375	WALL POCKET	MORNING GLORY DOUBLE	6.5H	1936-40	45
376F	WALL MASK	FEMALE LG	7.5H	1936	200
376M	WALL MASK	MALE LG	7.5H	1936	200
377	WALL POCKET	MORNING GLORY	7.5H	1936-50	35
378F	WALL MASK	FEMALE SM	4.0H	1936	175
378M	WALL MASK	MALE SM	4.0H	1936	175
379	WALL POCKET	DAISY	7.75D	1936-41	70

MOLD#	TYPE	NAME	SIZE	YEAR	$
379D	WALL POCKET	DAISY	7.75D	1936-41	80
380	VASE	RHYTHM MD	7.75H	1936-37	50
381	VASE	RHYTHM SM	5.5H	1936-37	45
382	BOWL	DAISY LG	12.25D	1936-38	55
383	BOWL	DAISY SM	9.5D	1936-38	45
384	CANDLEHOLDER	DAISY	4.5D	1936-38	40pr
385	BOWL	DAISY NUT DISH	3.5D	1936	25
386	ASHTRAY	DAISY	4.5D	1936-37	25
387	PLATE	DAISY SALAD	7.5D	1936-37	20
388	ANIMAL FIGURE	POUTER PIGEON	4.25H	1936-46	45
389	VASE	GERANIUM	7H	1936-37	55
390	VASE	M GLORY LG	10H	1936-39	50
391	VASE	M GLORY MD	7.75H	1936-38	45
392	VASE	M GLORY SM	5.5H	1936-38	40
393	BOWL	M GLORY	7D	1936-38	50
394	BOWL	MODERN BLM BT	8X10	1936-38	60
395	ARC DE FLEUR	ARC-DE-FLEUR	11.5D	1936-38	75set
396	FLOWER POT	LG	7SQ	1936-38	30
397	FLOWER POT	MD	5.75SQ	1936-38	25
398	FLOWER POT	SM	4.5SQ	1936-38	20
399	BOWL	DAISY SM	6.5D	1937-38	45
400	TEAPOT TILE	GEISHA	5SQ	1937-38	85
401	TEAPOT TILE	COOLIE	5SQ	1937-38	85
402	VASE	BOX	5.5H	1937-38	55
403	BOWL	CHAIN	8.5X12.5	1937-38	75
404	CANDLEHOLDER	TRIPLE CHAIN	3X8.5	1937-38	55pr
405	VASE	CROSSPATCH	8H	1937-38	55
406	CANDLEHOLDER	LEAF	3D	1937	75pr
407	BOWL	ROSE	6D	1937-38	50
408	BOWL	LEAF	6.5D	1937	75
409	BOWL	VOLUTE	6D	1937-39	65
410	VASE	VOLUTE SM	8H	1937-39	75
411	VASE	VOLUTE MD	10.5H	1937-40	100
412	VASE FLOOR	VOLUTE LG	15H	1937-40	150
413	BOWL	WREATH	12D	1937	75
414	CANDLEHOLDER	WREATH	4D	1937	65pr
415	PLATE	APPLE BLOSSOM	11.5D	1937	50
416	ANIMAL FIGURE	PEACOCK	7H	1937-38, 1942-46	55
417	VASE	SCROLL	8H	1937-38	80
418	VASE	TRI RIBBED	5H	1937-38	50
419	BOWL	RHYTHM	5D	1937	40
420	VASE	FERN LEAF	7.25H	1937-38	65
421	VASE	FERN LEAF	8.75H	1937-38	85
422	VASE	FERN LEAF	10.25H	1937-39	95
423	BOWL	FERN LEAF	7.25H	1937-38	85
424	BOWL	FERN LEAF	8.5H	1937-38	95
425	BOWL	FERN LEAF	10.5H	1937-38	110
426	FLOWER BOAT	FERN LEAF	13X4	1937-38	100
427	CANDLEHOLDER	FERN LEAF	5.5H	1937-38	50pr
428	BOOKEND	FERN LEAF	5.5H	1937-38	150pr
429	CANDLEHOLDER	FERN LEAF	8H	1937-38	75pr
430	PITCHER	FERN LEAF	8H	1937-38	125
431	WALL POCKET	FERN LEAF	7.5H	1937-38	110
432	FRUIT BOAT	FERN LEAF	15X6.5	1938-39	95
433	VASE FLOOR	FERN LEAF	15H	1937-39	145
434	CANDLEHOLDER	FERN LEAF BOAT	3X5.5	1938	75pr
435	WALL POCKET	FERN LEAF TRI	8W	1938-40	125
436	CANDLEHOLDER	FERN LEAF TRI	3X8	1938-39	95
437	BOWL	HAN PANSY	4X10.5	1938-50	10
438	VASE	HAN SQUARE	6SQ	1938-41	20
439	CANDLEHOLDER	HAN SINGLE	3SQ	1938	50pr
440	CANDLEHOLDER	HAN TRIPLE	3X7.5	1938	30pr
441	BOOKEND	HORSEHEADS	7H	1938-50	65pr
442	VASE	LAUREL SM	5.5H	1938-39	50
443	VASE	LAUREL LG	8H	1938-39	60
444	BOOKEND	DOLPHIN	5.75H	1938-49	40
444D	BOOKEND	DOLPHIN	5.75H	1938-49	65
445	VASE	LACED CUFF SM	8H	1938-39	50
446	VASE	LACED CUFF LG	10H	1938-39	60
447	CANDLEHOLDER	SUNBURST	8L	1938	50pr
448	WINDOW BOX	SUNBURST	9L	1938-39	40
449	CORNUCOPIA	SHELL	4.5H	1938-39, 1950	45
450	BOWL	ASTERS FLARE	11.5X7.5	1938-40	45
450D	BOWL	ASTERS FLARE	11.5X8	1939	65
451	CANDLEHOLDER	ASTERS DOUBLE	4.5H	1938-40	40pr
451D	CANDLE HOLDER	ASTERS DOUBLE	4.5H	1939	75pr
452	BOWL	ASTERS LG	15X9	1938-40	45
452D	BOWL	ASTERS LG	15X9	1939	65
453	VASE	ASTERS SM	8H	1938-39	40
453D	VASE	ASTERS SM	8H	1939	60
454	BOWL	ASTERS ROUND	6.5D	1938-40	65
454D	BOWL	ASTERS ROUND	6.75H	1939	85
455	VASE	ASTERS LG	11.5H	1938-40	50
455D	VASE	ASTERS LG	11.5H	1939	75
456	ASH TRAY	NEW MODE	5.75D	1939-48	30

MOLD#	TYPE	NAME	SIZE	YEAR	$
457	WALL POCKET	IONIC	9H	1939	100
458	VASE	LATTICE	5.5H	1939	45
459	VASE	LATTICE	10.25H	1939-41	55
460	BOWL	PANEL	8D	1939	125
461	CANDLE HOLDER	PANEL	2.5H	1939	90pr
462	VASE	RIBBON BOWL	4.5H	1939-50	15
463	VASE	STAR	7.5H	1939-50	25
464	VASE	MEDALLION	8H	1939-40	40
465	JAR	SNACK	7D	1939	95
466	VASE	WHEEL HANDLE	8H	1939-41	45
467	VASE	WREATH	8H	1939-40	65
468	VASE	BIRD	7.5H	1939-40	40
468D	VASE	BIRD	7.5H	1947-49	65
469	VASE	DUTCH BOY	8H	1939-40	75
470	VASE	DUTCH GIRL	8H	1939-40	75
471	COOKIE JAR	LITTLE OL'LADY	9H	1939-46	200
471DA	COOKIE JAR	LITTLE OL' LADY	9H	1942-47	275
471DB	COOKIE JAR	LITTLE OL' LADY	9H	1942-47	275
471DC	COOKIE JAR	LITTLE OL' LADY	9H	1942-47	275
472	VASE	REEDED	8H	1939	65
473	BOWL	COMBINATION	12X7	1939	120
474	CORNUCOPIA	SINGLE	5H	1939-50	20
475	WINDOW BOX	SM	7L	1939-40	25
476	WINDOW BOX	MD	10.5L	1939-50	30
477	WINDOW BOX	LG	13.5L	1939-41	35
478	BOWL	SCROLL SM	11.5L	1939-41	25
479	CANDLEHOLDER	SCROLL DOUBLE	4.5H	1939-50	20pr
480	BOWL	SCROLL LG	17.5L	1939-50	30
481	BOWL	IVY	12X7	1939-41	50
482	CORNUCOPIA	DOUBLE	11L	1939-50	25
483	VASE	PETITE BUD	8H	1939-40	35
483D	VASE	PETITE BUD	7.75H	1947-49	45
484	VASE	FAN	8.5	1939-50	15
485	VASE	ACANTHUS SM	8H	1939-40	45
486	VASE	ACANTHUS LG	11H	1939-50	30
487	VASE FLOOR	EGRET SM	14H	1939-40	150
488	ASHTRAY	BOX	4X3.25	1939-40	50
489	WALL POCKET	DUTCH BOY	10H	1939	125
490	WALL POCKET	DUTCH GIRL	10H	1939	125
491	VASE	FLOWER HOLDING	5H	1940-50	25
492	VASE	SMALL BOWL	4H	1940	350
493	WALL POCKET	DOUBLE	8.5H	1940	110
494	VASE	SHIP	7.5H	1940-46	30
494D	VASE	SHIP	7H	1947-49	45
495	COOKIE JAR	FAT BOY	8.25X 6	1940-46	700
496	VASE	HOLLYHOCK	7.5H	1940	30
496D	VASE	HOLLYHOCK	7H	1947-48	45
497	VASE	BLACKAMOOR	7.5H	1940	80
497 D	VASE	BLACKAMOOR	7.5H	1940	150
498	WINDOW BOX	HAN LG	14.5L	1940-41	20
499	BOOKEND	TROJAN HEAD	7.5H	1940-41	125ea
500	BOWL	SHELL LG	15L	1940-49	30
501	BOWL	SHELL MD	10.5L	1940-48	25
502	BOWL	SHELL SM	7L	1940-41	30
503	CANDLEHOLDER	SHELL SINGLE	4X3.5	1940-50	20pr
504	VASE	SHELL PLANTING	7.5H	1940-46	45
505	CANDLEHOLDER	SHELL DOUBLE	4H	1940-49	25pr
506	BOWL	SHELL	5.5H	1940-50	25
506X	BOWL	SHELL HANGING	5.5H		25
507	VASE	SHELL OVAL	7.5H	1940-50	25
508	WALL POCKET	SHELL	7H	1940	90
509	ASHTRAY	ELEPHANT	5.5D	1940-41	150
510	ASHTRAY	DONKEY	5.5D	1940-41	150
511	VASE	IONIC	8L	1940-41	35
512	VASE	SWIRL SM	7H	1940-50	25
513	VASE	SWIRL MD	9H	1940-50	35
514	VASE	SWIRL LG	11H	1940-50	50
515	VASE	ABBEY	7H	1940-50	25
516	VASE	ACADIA	7H	1940-50	25
517	VASE	ARDEN	7H	1940-50	30
518	BOWL	ROUND BULB	12D	1940-50	15
519	BOWL	ROUND BULB	9D	1940-50	15
520	VASE	BADEN	9H	1940-48	30
521	VASE	BALI	9H	1940-41	90
522	VASE	BARRE	9H	1940-50	30
523	BOWL	HAN OBLONG	14X9	1940	30
524	VASE FLOOR	EGRET LG	17.5H	1940-50	185
524A	VASE FLOOR	EGRET, SAND JAR	18H	1940-50	220
525	BOWL	FLARE OBLONG	10X7	1940-50	15
526	BOWL	BULB OBLONG	10X6	1940-50	15
527	BOWL	HIBISCUS SM	10D	1941-48	35
528	BOWL	HIBISCUS LG	15D	1941-49	45
529	BOWL	TI LEAF	16X5	1941-46	40
530	BOWL	TRAVELER'S PALM	16X6.5	1941-46	45
531	BOWL	FLEUR DE LIS	14X9	1941	45
532	BOWL	SCROLL MD	14.5L	1941-50	30
533	BOWL	SHELL	12L	1941-50	25

MOLD#	TYPE	NAME	SIZE	YEAR	$
534	VASE	BOYNE	9H	1941-46	40
535	VASE	BERNE	9H	1941-46	45
536	BOWL	REGENCY	9L	1941-50	15
537	VASE	TASSEL	9H	1941	65
538	URN	WREATH	9H	1941-46, 1950	25
539	URN	REGENCY	7H	1941	25
540	BOWL	FLARE	11.5X8	1941	45
541	BOWL	OVAL LG	15X9	1941	40
542	BOWL	OVAL BULB LG	15X9	1941-50	20
543	BOWL	ROUND BULB SM	5.5D	1941-46	15
543D	BOX	GERANIUM	3.25H	1947	75
544	BOWL	STREAMLINER SM	9X6	1941-50	20
545	BOWL	STREAMLINER MD	8X11	1941-50	10
546	BOWL	STREAMLINER LG	9X14.5	1941-46	15
547	BOWL	IRREGULAR	7X10	1941-46	15
548	BOWL	ROUND LG	14D	1941	35
549	COOKIE JAR	HIPPO	8HX7D	1941-47	250
549A	COOKIE JAR	HIPPO	8HX7D	1942-47	350
549B	COOKIE JAR	HIPPO	8HX7D	1942-47	550
549C	COOKIE JAR	HIPPO	8HX7D	1942-47	350
550	VASE	FLUTED	11H	1941-50	30
551	ASHTRAY	OCTAGONAL	7SQ	1941-46	25
552	VASE	SQUATTY	8.5D	1941-48	45
553	VASE	GRECIAN	13H	1941-47	55
554	VASE	RIBBED	9H	1941-46	50
555	ASHTRAY	ROUND	8D	1941-46	25
556	VASE	LARGE	12.5H	1941-46	55
557	VASE	DRAPED	11H	1941-48	45
558	CACHE POT	SM	4.75	1947	25
558D	CACHE POT	SM	4.75D	1942-46	35
559	CACHE POT	MD	5.5H	1947-46	25
559D	CACHE POT	MD	5.5H	1942-46	35
560	CACHE POT	LG	6.5H	1947	30
560D	CACHE POT	LG	6.5H	1942-46	45
561	COOKIE JAR	BABY	11HX8D	1941-46	600
561-71	COOKIE JAR	SPECIAL	8D	1942-46	UD
562	ANIMAL FIGURE	GULL	5H	1942-46	75
563	URN	URN	9H	1947-48	35
563D	VASE	URN	9H	1942-46	50
564	BOWL	SCALLOP	11L	1942-50	15
565	CORNUCOPIA	HIGH	7H	1947-48	20
565D	CORNUCOPIA	HIGH	7H	1942-46	40
566	VASE	SCALLOP	9H	1947-48	25
566D	VASE	SCALLOP	9H	1942-46	45
567	VASE		5H	1947	30
567D	VASE		5H	1942-46	40
568	COMPOTE	MINT	6D	1942-47	25
569	CORNUCOPIA	LOW	8L	1947-48	15
569D	CORNUCOPIA	LOW	8L	1942-46	25
570	WINDOW BOX		10L	1947-50	15
570D	WINDOW BOX		10L	1942-46	20
571	ANIMAL FIGURE	GOOSE SITTING	5H	1942-47	35
571D	ANIMAL FIGURE	GOOSE SITTING	5H	1947	60
572	ANIMAL FIGURE	PELICAN	5H	1942-46	40
572D	ANIMAL FIGURE	PELICAN	5.5H	1947	60
573	ANIMAL FIGURE	PENGUIN	5.5H	1942-46	45
573D	ANIMAL FIGURE	PENGUIN	5H	1947	65
574	ANIMAL FIGURE	HERON	5.25H	1942-46	35
574D	ANIMAL FIGURE	HERON	5.25H	1947-49	60
575	CANDLEHOLDER	DOUBLE	5H	1942-50	20pr
576	WINDOW BOX	LG	12.25L	1947-50	25
577	VASE	PILLOW	7H	1947-50	20
578	CANDLEHOLDER	VICTORY BOAT	U/C		100
579	CANDLEHOLDER	ALADDIN LAMP	U/C		100
580D	BOX	BUTTERFLY	4.75D	1947	85
581	CORNUCOPIA	DOUBLE	8.25H	1947-48	40
582D	BASKET	FLOWER	8H	1947-48	45
583	CORNUCOPIA	TRIPLE	9D	1947-48	40
584	VASE	BOOT	8H	1947	45
585D	BOX	ROSEBUD	4.5D	1947-48	85
586D	WALL VASE	CALLA	9H	1947-48	40
587	WALL BRACKET	CHERUB	7.5H	1947	75
588D	COOKIE JAR	MONEY BAG	7.5H	1947-50	100
589	WALL BRACKET	ACANTHUS	7H	1947	65
590D	WALL POCKET	IVY	7H	1947	65
591	VASE	PLEAT	10H	1947-48	35
592	BOWL	LOW OVAL	10.5L	1947-50	20
593	VASE	BOW KNOT	9H	1947-48	35
594	VASE	HOUR GLASS	9H	1947	30
595	BOOKEND	QUILL PEN	8.25	1947-48	175 pr
596D	VASE	SEAHORSE	8H	1947-48	60
597	VASE	TRUMPET	9H	1947	45
598D	VASE	ROSETTE	7.25H	1947-48	45
599	VASE	QUILTED	9H	1947-50	55
600	VASE	LAUREL	12H	1947-49	90
601D	WALL POCKET	BUTTERFLY	8.5H	1947-49	110

MOLD#	TYPE	NAME	SIZE	YEAR	$
602D	COOKIE JAR	HOBBY HORSE	10.5H	1947-50	295
603	VASE FLOOR	GRECIAN	15H	1947-49	150
604D	VASE	TULIP	6H	1947-48	75
605D	ANIMAL FIGURE	KANGAROO	7H	1947	200
606	JAR	ELEPHANT	9.75H	1947	200
607D	BOX	CANDY CANE	4.5H	1947-48	100
608	BOX	ELEPHANT	6L	1947-48	175
609D	JAR	PELICAN	6.5H	1947	175
610	BOWL	SHELL DEEP	9D	1947-48	45
611D	COOKIE JAR	JACK IN THE BOX	11H	1947-49	500
612	BOX	LILY TRAY BOX	9.5L	1947	135
613	VASE FLOOR	GRECIAN PITCHER	15H	1947	150
614	CANDLEHOLDER	CANDLE REFLECTOR	6.5H	1947	110pr
615	ASHTRAY	CHIC	4D	1947-48	30
616D	VASE	CACTUS	6.5H	1947-50	65
625	VASE	RIBBED	6.5H	1948	50
626	VASE	TAPER	6H	1948-49	50
627	CACHE POT	CACHE POT	6H	1948-49	45
628D	VASE	IRIS	8H	1948-49	60
629D	VASE	POPPY	6.5H	1948-49	80
630	VASE	HANDLED	9H	1948-49	50
631	VASE	SQUARE	8H	1948-49	45
632	VASE	ANCHOR	7.5H	1948-49	40
633	BOWL	TRAY	10L	1948-50	20
634	VASE	HEIRLOOM	6.5H	1948	45
635	VASE	POCKET	6H	1948	45
636D	VASE	TRIANGULAR	6.25H	1948	55
637	VASE	OBLONG	9H	1948-50	45
638	COMPOTE	COMPOTE	4H	1948-50	30
639	VASE	CALLA	8.5H	1948	40
640	WALL POCKET	TRIAD	8X5.5	1948-50	40
641	BOWL	WHIRL	6.5H	1948	35
642	BOWL	TULIP	6.5H	1948-49	70
643	CORNUCOPIA	LOW	9.5L	1948-49	50
644	BOWL	RIPPLE	6H	1948-49	25
645	BOWL	CONTOUR	10.75L	1948-50	20
646	CORNUCOPIA	HIGH	7H	1948-49	60
647	URN	TALL	13.5	1948-50	50
648	WALL VASE	ACANTHUS	8.75H	1948-50	65
649	WALL BRACKET	ACANTHUS	8.75H	1948	65
650	BOOKEND	SCOTTY	7.5H	1948	200 pr
651D	COOKIE JAR	CHOO CHOO	7.5H	1948-50	225
652D	PLANTER	PUPPY	6.75L	1948-49	50
653D	COOKIE JAR	CLOCK	9H	1948-50	130
654	VASE	TULIP	6.5H	1948-49	75
655D	PLANTER	DUTCH SHOE	5L	1948	45
656	PLANTER	SQUARE	3.5H	1948-50	15
657	ANIMAL FIGURE	SWORDFISH	4.5H	1948-50	55
657D	ANIMAL FIGURE	SWORDFISH	4.25H	1948-49	75
658	BOWL	RIBBED	10L	1948-50	25
659	VASE	HACKNEY	8.5H	1948-49	45
660	ASHTRAY	LEAF	5.5D	1948-50	20
661	ANIMAL FIGURE	SWAN	3.75H	1948-50	55
661D	ANIMAL FIGURE	SWAN	3.25H	1948	85
662D	COOKIE JAR	MISS MUFFET	11H	1949-50	275
663D	COOKIE JAR	HUMPTY DUMPTY	10.5H	1949-50	275
664D	COOKIE JAR	PINEAPPLE	10.5H	1949-50	200
665D	COOKIE JAR	WIGWAM	11H	1949	900
666D	JAM SET	4 PIECE	3.5H	1949-50	100
667	PLANTER	GOURD	5.5H	1949-50	20
668D	PLANTER	DAFFODIL	5.25H	1949	75
669	PLANTER	DONKEY	7.5H	1949-50	75
670	PLANTER	POOCH	4H	1949-50	55
671	PLANTER	RAM	4H	1949-50	40
672	PLANTER	FAWN	5H	1949-50	45
673	PLANTER	BURRO	4.5H	1949-50	45
674D	COOKIE JAR	PUMPKIN	8H	1949-50	425
675D	WALL VASE	MATCH BOX	5.5H	1949-50	90
676D	WALL VASE	BOOK	6.5H	1949	100
677D	COOKIE JAR	DAISY	8H	1949-50	95
678D	COOKIE JAR	WINDMILL	10.5H	1949	400
679	GREASE JAR	DAISY	4.5H	1949-50	35
680	SALT & PEPPER	DAISY	4H	1949-50	25pr
681	SUGAR BOWL	DAISY	3H	1949-50	20
682	CREAM PITCHER	DAISY	2.5H	1949-50	20
683	TEA POT	DAISY	6.25	1949-50	65
684	BOWL	CRESCENT	5W	1949	15
685	BOWL	RIBBED LG	13.75L	1949	25
686	BOWL	CONTOUR LG	13.25L	1949	25
687	BOWL	PLANTER	5SQ	1949-50	15
688	CANDLEHOLDER	RIBBED	1.75H	1949	25pr
689	CANDLEHOLDER	CONTOUR	1.75H	1949	25pr
690D	RANGE SET	DAISY	3PIECES	1949-50	75
691D	TEA SET	DAISY	3PIECES	1949-50	125
692D	COOKIE JAR	WITCH	11.5	1950	1500
693D	COOKIE JAR	LITTLE GIRL	9.5H	1950	125
694D	COOKIE JAR	BO PEEP	12H	1950	375

MOLD#	TYPE	NAME	SIZE	YEAR	$
695D	COOKIE JAR	MOTHER GOOSE	12H	1950	425
696D	COOKIE JAR	THREE BEARS	8.75H	1950	250
697D	COOKIE JAR	FLORAL/PLAID	8.5H	1950	110
698	VASE	CHINESE TERRACE	6H	1950	45
699D	WALL VASE	APRON	6H	1950	115
700D	BOWL	PINEAPPLE	14.75L	1950	90
701	PLANTER	CHINESE SQUARE	4.75H	1950	50
702D	STRING HOLDER	CHINESE FACE	5.5H	1950	175
703	VASE	SLANT TOP	9.5H	1950	85
704	PLANTER	GAZELLE	4.75H	1950	45
705	VASE	MODERN	8H	1950	45
706	VASE	OAK LEAF	9.25H	1950	55
706D	VASE	OAK LEAF	9.25H	1950	70
707	BOWL	CRADLE PLANTER	6.5L	1950	20
708	VASE	SQUARE LEAF	9H	1950	40
708D	VASE	SQUARE LEAF	9H	1950	80
709	BOWL	IRREGULAR	13.5L	1950	25
710	PLANTER	DRAPE	7L	1950	45
711	WALL VASE	CARRIAGE LAMP	10H	1950	80
712D	STRINGHOLDER	MOUSE	8.5H	1950	175
713	BOWL	STAR CONSOLE	10D	1950	55
714	CANDLEHOLDER	STAR	4.25	1950	45pr
715D	PLATE	BAMBOO CONSOLE	10.5D	1950	175
716D	CANDLEHOLDER	BAMBOO SQUARE	3.5SQ	1950	50pr
717	VASE	MRS. BIDWELL		1950	UTD
718	VASE	BASKET WEAVE		1950	UTD
719	CANDLEHOLDER	REDESIGN OF 479		1950	UTD
720	BOWL	REDESIGN OF 480	18L	1950	UTD
721	WINDOW BOX		12.5L	1950	UTD
722	BOWL	OBLONG FRUIT	14.5L	1950	UTD
723	N/D				
724	WALL POCKET	LEAF	10X5.5L	1950	UTD
725	VASE	ROUND		1950	UTD
726	PLANTER	CART	5X5SQ	1950	UTD
727	VASE	MRS. ANDREWS		1950	
728	N/D				
729	WINDOW BOX	SCROLL END		1950	UTD
730	VASE	MODERN BUD	8.5H	1950	UTD
731	N/D				
732	PLANTER	SQUARE FLUTED	6SQ	1950	UTD
733	BOWL	RIGHT ANGLE	5X5X5	1950	UTD
734	CANDLEHOLDER	CUBE	2.5SQ	1950	UTD
735	N/D				
A1	VASE	WHAT NOT	3.5H	1940-41	65
A2	VASE	WHAT NOT	3.5H	1940-41	65
A3	VASE	WHAT NOT	3.5H	1940-41	65
A4	VASE	WHAT NOT	3.5H	1940-41	65
A5	VASE	WHAT NOT	3.5H	1940-41	65
A6	VASE	WHAT NOT	3.5H	1940-41	65
B1	VASE	WHAT NOT	5H	1940-41	75
B2	VASE	WHAT NOT	5H	1940-41	75
B3	VASE	WHAT NOT	5H	1940-41	75
B4	VASE	WHAT NOT	5H	1940-41	75
B5	VASE	WHAT NOT	5H	1940-41	75
B6	VASE	WHAT NOT	5H	1940-41	75
C1	VASE	WHAT NOT	4.5H	1940-41	95
C2	VASE	WHAT NOT	4.5H	1940-41	75
C3	VASE	WHAT NOT	4.5H	1940-41	75
C4	VASE	WHAT NOT	4.5H	1940-41	75
C5	VASE	WHAT NOT	4.5H	1940-41	75
C6	VASE	WHAT NOT	4.5H	1940-41	75
G1	VASE GARDEN	TALL OIL JAR	24HX14.5D	1938-50	275
G2	VASE GARDEN	SQUATTY PALM	19.5X18	1939-50	240
G3	VASE FLOOR	ROPE LG	18H	1939-50	190
G4	VASE FLOOR	ROPE SM	14H	1939-50	175
P4	JARDINIERE	LA FLEUR	3D	1941-50	15
P5	JARDINIERE	LA FLEUR	4D	1941-50	15
P6	JARDINIERE	LA FLEUR	5D	1941-50	20
P7	JARDINIERE	LA FLEUR	6D	1941-50	25
P8	JARDINIERE	LA FLEUR	7D	1941-50	25
RE1	REFRIGERATOR	WATER JUG	2 QT	1940	85
RE2	REFRIGERATOR	OBLONG LEFT OVR		1940	65
RE3	REFRIGERATOR	SQUARE LEFT OVR		1940	65
RE4	REFRIGERATOR	BUTTER DISH		1940	75
RE5	REFRIGERATOR	CASSEROLE	8L	1940	75
RE6	REFRIGERATOR	ROUND LEFT OVER	6D	1940	60
RE7	REFRIGERATOR	ROUND LEFT OVER	5D	1940	55
RE8	REFRIGERATOR	ROUND LEFT OVER	4D	1940	50

ORGANIZED BY MOLD TYPE

MOLD#	TYPE	NAME	SIZE	YEAR	$
99	ANIMAL FIGURE	GOOSE LEANING	2.5H	1948-50	40
571	ANIMAL FIGURE	GOOSE SITTING	5H	1942-47	35
571D	ANIMAL FIGURE	GOOSE SITTING	5H	1947	60
98	ANIMAL FIGURE	GOOSE UPRIGHT	5H	1948-50	40
562	ANIMAL FIGURE	GULL	5H	1942-46	75
574	ANIMAL FIGURE	HERON	5.25H	1942-46	35
574D	ANIMAL FIGURE	HERON	5.25H	1947-49	60
605D	ANIMAL FIGURE	KANGAROO	7H	1947	200
416	ANIMAL FIGURE	PEACOCK	7H	1937-38, 1942-46	55
572	ANIMAL FIGURE	PELICAN	5H	1942-46	40
572D	ANIMAL FIGURE	PELICAN	5.5H	1947	60
573	ANIMAL FIGURE	PENGUIN	5.5H	1942-46	45
573D	ANIMAL FIGURE	PENGUIN	5H	1947	65
388	ANIMAL FIGURE	POUTER PIGEON	4.25H	1936-46	45
661	ANIMAL FIGURE	SWAN	3.75H	1948-50	55
661D	ANIMAL FIGURE	SWAN	3.25H	1948	85
657	ANIMAL FIGURE	SWORDFISH	4.5H	1948-50	55
657D	ANIMAL FIGURE	SWORDFISH	4.25H	1948-49	75
395	ARC DE FLEUR	ARC-DE-FLEUR	11.5D	1936-38	75set
456	ASH TRAY	NEW MODE	5.75D	1939-48	30
306	ASHTRAY	ABINGDON	8X3	1934-36	55
488	ASHTRAY	BOX	4X3.25	1939-40	50
615	ASHTRAY	CHIC	4D	1947-48	30
386	ASHTRAY	DAISY	4.5D	1936-37	25
510	ASHTRAY	DONKEY	5.5D	1940-41	150
356	ASHTRAY	DUO	6.75X3.5	1936	35
509	ASHTRAY	ELEPHANT	5.5D	1940-41	150
326	ASHTRAY	GREEK	4.25X3	1934-36	65
369	ASHTRAY	GUARD	5SQ	1936	35
660	ASHTRAY	LEAF	5.5D	1948-50	20
551	ASHTRAY	OCTAGONAL	7SQ	1941-46	25
371	ASHTRAY	PETITE	4D	1936-37	25
317	ASHTRAY	ROUND	5D	1934-37	25
555	ASHTRAY	ROUND	8D	1941-46	25
316	ASHTRAY	TROJAN	5X3.5	1934-36	65
334	ASHTRAY	UTILITY	5.5D	1935-37	20
582D	BASKET	FLOWER	8H	1947-48	45
370	BOOKEND	CACTUS	6H	1936-38	100pr
374	BOOKEND	CACTUS PLANTER	7H	1936-38	125
363	BOOKEND	COLT	6H	1935-38	375pr
444	BOOKEND	DOLPHIN	5.75H	1938-49	40
444D	BOOKEND	DOLPHIN	5.75H	1938-49	65
428	BOOKEND	FERN LEAF	5.5H	1937-38	150pr
441	BOOKEND	HORSEHEADS	7H	1938-50	65pr
595	BOOKEND	QUILL PEN	8.25	1947-48	175 pr
321	BOOKEND	RUSSIAN	6.5 H	1934-40	300pr
650	BOOKEND	SCOTTY	7.5H	1948	200 pr
305	BOOKEND	SEAGULL	6 H	1934-46	150pr
499	BOOKEND	TROJAN HEAD	7.5H	1940-41	125ea
450	BOWL	ASTERS FLARE	11.5X7.5	1938-40	45
450D	BOWL	ASTERS FLARE	11.5X8	1939	65
452	BOWL	ASTERS, LG	15X9	1938-40	45
452D	BOWL	ASTERS, LG	15X9	1939	65
454	BOWL	ASTERS ROUND	6.5D	1938-40	65
454D	BOWL	ASTERS ROUND	6.75H	1939	85
526	BOWL	BULB OBLONG	10X6	1940-50	15
403	BOWL	CHAIN	8.5X12.5	1937-38	75
345	BOWL	CHINESE OVAL	9X11	1935-37	90
127	BOWL	CLASSIC, LG	14X6.5	1940-41	50
125	BOWL	CLASSIC, SM	11X6.5	1940-41	50
473	BOWL	COMBINATION	12X7	1939	120
645	BOWL	CONTOUR	10.75L	1948-50	20
686	BOWL	CONTOUR, LG	13.25L	1949	25
341	BOWL	COUPE SOUP	5.5D	1935	45
707	BOWL	CRADLE PLANTER	6.5L	1950	20
684	BOWL	CRESCENT	5W	1949	15
382	BOWL	DAISY, LG	12.25D	1936-38	55
385	BOWL	DAISY NUT DISH	3.5D	1936	25
383	BOWL	DAISY, SM	9.5D	1936-38	45
399	BOWL	DAISY, SM	6.5D	1937-38	45
423	BOWL	FERN LEAF	7.25H	1937-38	85
424	BOWL	FERN LEAF	8.5H	1937-38	95
425	BOWL	FERN LEAF	10.5H	1937-38	110
540	BOWL	FLARE	11.5X8	1941	45
525	BOWL	FLARE OBLONG	10X7	1940-50	15
531	BOWL	FLEUR DE LIS	14X9	1941	45
311	BOWL	FLOWER	6.5D	1934-36	40
523	BOWL	HAN OBLONG	14X9	1940	30
437	BOWL	HAN PANSY	4X10.5	1938-50	10
528	BOWL	HIBISCUS, LG	15D	1941-49	45
527	BOWL	HIBISCUS, SM	10D	1941-48	35
547	BOWL	IRREGULAR	7X10	1941-46	15
709	BOWL	IRREGULAR	13.5L	1950	25
481	BOWL	IVY	12X7	1939-41	50
153	BOWL	LA FLEUR	6D	1938-39	12
154	BOWL	LA FLEUR	8D	1938-39	12
155	BOWL	LA FLEUR	10D	1938-39	12
156	BOWL	LA FLEUR	8L	1938	15
157	BOWL	LA FLEUR	10L	1938	12
408	BOWL	LEAF	6.5D	1937	75
592	BOWL	LOW OVAL	10.5L	1947-50	20
393	BOWL	M GLORY	7D	1936-38	50
394	BOWL	MODERN BLM BT	8X10	1936-38	60
362	BOWL	MONOFORM	6D	1935-36	50
722	BOWL	OBLONG FRUIT	14.5L	1950	UTD
542	BOWL	OVAL BULB, LG	15X9	1941-50	20
541	BOWL	OVAL, LG	15X9	1941	40
460	BOWL	PANEL	8D	1939	125
700D	BOWL	PINEAPPLE	14.75L	1950	90
687	BOWL	PLANTER	5SQ	1949-50	15
720	BOWL	REDESIGN OF 480	18L	1950	UTD
536	BOWL	REGENCY	9L	1941-50	15
419	BOWL	RHYTHM	5D	1937	40
658	BOWL	RIBBED	10L	1948-50	25
685	BOWL	RIBBED, LG	13.75L	1949-50	25
733	BOWL	RIGHT ANGLE	5X5X5	1950	UTD
644	BOWL	RIPPLE	6H	1948-49	25
407	BOWL	ROSE	6D	1937-38	50
518	BOWL	ROUND BULB	12D	1940-50	15
519	BOWL	ROUND BULB	9D	1940-50	15
543	BOWL	ROUND BULB, SM	5.5D	1941-46	15
548	BOWL	ROUND, LG	14D	1941	35
313	BOWL	SALAD BOWL	10.5 D	1934-36	75
564	BOWL	SCALLOP	11L	1942-50	15
480	BOWL	SCROLL, LG	17.5L	1939-50	30
532	BOWL	SCROLL, MD	14.5L	1941-50	30
478	BOWL	SCROLL, SM	11.5L	1939-41	25
9701	BOWL	SHALLOW OBLONG		1950	30
9700	BOWL	SHALLOW OVAL		1950	30
9699	BOWL	SHALLOW SQUARE		1950	30
506	BOWL	SHELL	5.5H	1940-50	25
533	BOWL	SHELL	12L	1941-50	25
610	BOWL	SHELL DEEP	9D	1947-48	45
506X	BOWL	SHELL HANGING	5.5H		25
500	BOWL	SHELL, LG	15L	1940-49	30
501	BOWL	SHELL, MD	10.5L	1940-48	25
502	BOWL	SHELL, SM	7L	1940-41	30
338	BOWL	SQ COVERED	4.75SQ	1935	65
336	BOWL	SQUARE	9SQ	1935-41	60
713	BOWL	STAR CONSOLE	10D	1950	55
546	BOWL	STREAMLINER, LG	9X14.5	1941-46	15
545	BOWL	STREAMLINER, MD	8X11	1941-50	10
544	BOWL	STREAMLINER, SM	9X6	1941-50	20
529	BOWL	TI LEAF	16X5	1941-46	40
530	BOWL	TRAVELER'S PALM	16X6.5	1941-46	45
633	BOWL	TRAY	10L	1948-50	20
361	BOWL	TRIFORM	8X14.5	1935-37	65
642	BOWL	TULIP	6.5H	1948-49	70
409	BOWL	VOLUTE	6D	1937-39	65
641	BOWL	WHIRL	6.5H	1948	35
413	BOWL	WREATH	12D	1937	75
580D	BOX	BUTTERFLY	4.75D	1947	85
607D	BOX	CANDY CANE	4.5H	1947-48	100
608	BOX	ELEPHANT	6L	1947-48	175
543D	BOX	GERANIUM	3.25H	1947	75
612	BOX	LILY TRAY BOX	9.5L	1947	135
585D	BOX	ROSEBUD	4.5D	1947-48	85
348	BOX (CIGARETTE)	TRIX	4.75X3.75	1935-37 1947	50
354	BOX	TRIXTRA	2X3	1935-37	35
627	CACHE POT	CACHE POT	6H	1948-49	45
560	CACHE POT	LG	6.5H	1947	30
560D	CACHE POT	LG	6.5H	1942-46	45
559	CACHE POT	MD	5.5H	1947-48	25
559D	CACHE POT	MD	5.5H	1942-46	35
558	CACHE POT	SM	4.75	1947	25
558D	CACHE POT	SM	4.75D	1942-46	35
451D	CANDLE HOLDER	ASTERS DOUBLE	4.5	1939	75pr
461	CANDLE HOLDER	PANEL	2.5H	1939	90pr
323	CANDLE HOLDER	ROPE	3.75 D	1934-36	40pr
579	CANDLEHOLDER	ALADDIN LAMP	U/C		100
451	CANDLEHOLDER	ASTERS DOUBLE	4.5	1938-40	40pr
716D	CANDLEHOLDER	BAMBOO SQUARE	3.5SQ	1950	50pr
614	CANDLEHOLDER	CANDLE REFLECTOR	6.5H	1947	110pr
126	CANDLEHOLDER	CLASSIC, SINGLE	2X3.5	1940-41	45pr
689	CANDLEHOLDER	CONTOUR	1.75H	1949	25pr
734	CANDLEHOLDER	CUBE	2.5SQ	1950	UTD
384	CANDLEHOLDER	DAISY	4.5D	1936-38	40pr
575	CANDLEHOLDER	DOUBLE	5H	1942-50	20pr
355	CANDLEHOLDER	EIFEL	4.75H	1935-36	100pr
427	CANDLEHOLDER	FERN LEAF	5.5H	1937-38	50pr

429	CANDLEHOLDER	FERN LEAF	8H	1937-38	75pr
434	CANDLEHOLDER	FERN LEAF BOAT	3X5.5	1938	75pr
436	CANDLEHOLDER	FERN LEAF TRI	3X8	1938-39	95
439	CANDLEHOLDER	HAN SINGLE	3SQ	1938	50pr
440	CANDLEHOLDER	HAN TRIPLE	3X7.5	1938	30pr
336A	CANDLEHOLDER	HURRICANE (W/GLASS)	11H	1939-41	45pr
158	CANDLEHOLDER	LA FLEUR	2HX3.5D	1938-39	15
406	CANDLEHOLDER	LEAF	3D	1937	75pr
368C	CANDLEHOLDER	MODERN, LG	4H	1936-38	35pr
368B	CANDLEHOLDER	MODERN, MD	3H	1936-38	35pr
368A	CANDLEHOLDER	MODERN, SM	2H	1936-38	35pr
360	CANDLEHOLDER	QUATRAIN	3SQ	1935-36	50pr
719	CANDLEHOLDER	REDESIGN OF 479		1950	UTD
688	CANDLEHOLDER	RIBBED	1.75H	1949	25pr
479	CANDLEHOLDER	SCROLL DOUBLE	4.5H	1939-50	20pr
505	CANDLEHOLDER	SHELL DOUBLE	4H	1940-49	25pr
503	CANDLEHOLDER	SHELL SINGLE	4X3.5	1940-50	20pr
714	CANDLEHOLDER	STAR	4.25	1950	45pr
447	CANDLEHOLDER	SUNBURST	8L	1938	50pr
404	CANDLEHOLDER	TRIPLE CHAIN	3X8.5	1937-38	55pr
578	CANDLEHOLDER	VICTORY BOAT	U/C		100
414	CANDLEHOLDER	WREATH	4D	1937	65pr
349	CHALICE	CHALICE	5.5H	1935-37	100
03905B	CHESSMAN	BISHOP	4.5H	1937	95
03905C	CHESSMAN	CASTLE	4H	1937	95
03905K	CHESSMAN	KING	5.5H	1937	95
03905N	CHESSMAN	KNIGHT	5H	1937	95
03905P	CHESSMAN	PAWN	3.5H	1937	95
03905Q	CHESSMAN	QUEEN	5H	1937	95
638	COMPOTE	COMPOTE	4H	1948-50	30
568	COMPOTE	MINT	6D	1942-47	25
561	COOKIE JAR	BABY	11HX8D	1941-46	600
694D	COOKIE JAR	BO PEEP	12H	1950	375
651D	COOKIE JAR	CHOO CHOO	7.5H	1948-50	225
653D	COOKIE JAR	CLOCK	9H	1948-50	130
677D	COOKIE JAR	DAISY	8H	1949-50	95
495	COOKIE JAR	FAT BOY	8.25X 6	1940-46	700
697D	COOKIE JAR	FLORAL/PLAID	8.5H	1950	110
549	COOKIE JAR	HIPPO	8HX7D	1941-47	250
549A	COOKIE JAR	HIPPO	8HX7D	1942-47	350
549B	COOKIE JAR	HIPPO	8HX7D	1942-47	550
549C	COOKIE JAR	HIPPO	8HX7D	1942-47	350
602D	COOKIE JAR	HOBBY HORSE	10.5H	1947-50	295
663D	COOKIE JAR	HUMPTY DUMPTY	10.5H	1949-50	275
611D	COOKIE JAR	JACK IN THE BOX	11H	1947-49	500
693D	COOKIE JAR	LITTLE GIRL	9.5H	1950	125
471DA	COOKIE JAR	LITTLE OL' LADY	9H	1942-47	275
471DB	COOKIE JAR	LITTLE OL' LADY	9H	1942-47	275
471DC	COOKIE JAR	LITTLE OL' LADY	9H	1942-47	275
471	COOKIE JAR	LITTLE OL'LADY	9H	1939-46	200
662D	COOKIE JAR	MISS MUFFET	11H	1949-50	275
588D	COOKIE JAR	MONEY BAG	7.5H	1947-50	100
695D	COOKIE JAR	MOTHER GOOSE	12H	1950	425
664D	COOKIE JAR	PINEAPPLE	10.5H	1949-50	200
674D	COOKIE JAR	PUMPKIN	8H	1949-50	425
561-71	COOKIE JAR	SPECIAL	8D	1942-46	UD
696D	COOKIE JAR	THREE BEARS	8.75H	1950	250
665D	COOKIE JAR	WIGWAM	11H	1949	900
678D	COOKIE JAR	WINDMILL	10.5H	1949	400
692D	COOKIE JAR	WITCH	11.5	1950	1500
303	CORNUCOPIA	CORNUCOPIA	7.5H	1934-36	60
482	CORNUCOPIA	DOUBLE	11L	1939-50	25
581	CORNUCOPIA	DOUBLE	8.25H	1947-48	40
565	CORNUCOPIA	HIGH	7H	1947-48	20
565D	CORNUCOPIA	HIGH	7H	1942-46	40
646	CORNUCOPIA	HIGH	7H	1948-49	60
569	CORNUCOPIA	LOW	8L	1947-48	15
569D	CORNUCOPIA	LOW	8L	1942-46	25
643	CORNUCOPIA	LOW	9.5L	1948-49	50
449	CORNUCOPIA	SHELL	4.5H	1938-39, 1950	45
474	CORNUCOPIA	SINGLE	5H	1939-50	20
583	CORNUCOPIA	TRIPLE	9D	1947-48	40
682	CREAM PITCHER	DAISY	2.5H	1949-50	20
337	DESERT DISH	SQUARE	5SQ	1935	40
347	FLOWER POT	EGG & DART	7.25D	1935-37	15
366	FLOWER POT	EGG & DART, MD	5.25H	1936-37	20
367	FLOWER POT	EGG & DART, SM	4.5H	1936-37	20
426	FLOWER BOAT	FERN LEAF	13X4	1937-38	100
358	FLOWER POT	IONIC	5H	1935-37	30
358A	FLOWER POT	IONIC, LG	10.5D	1937	40
149	FLOWER POT	LA FLEUR	3H	1938-50	15
149D	FLOWER POT	LA FLEUR	3H	1938-50	25
150	FLOWER POT	LA FLEUR	4H	1938-46	15
150D	FLOWER POT	LA FLEUR	4H	1938-46	30
151	FLOWER POT	LA FLEUR	5H	1947-50	15
151D	FLOWER POT	LA FLEUR	5H	1947-50	35
152	FLOWER POT	LA FLEUR	6H	1938-50	15
152D	FLOWER POT	LA FLEUR	6H	1938-50	45
396	FLOWER POT	LG	7SQ	1936-38	30
359	FLOWER POT	MART	3.5H	1935-37	20
397	FLOWER POT	MD	5.75SQ	1936-38	25
346	FLOWER POT	RING STAND	5.5D	1935-36	15
398	FLOWER POT	SM	4.5SQ	1936-38	20
432	FRUIT BOAT	FERN LEAF	15X6.5	1938-39	95
322	GOBLET	SWEDISH	6.5 H	1934-36, 1947	70
679	GREASE JAR	DAISY	4.5H	1949-50	35
666D	JAM SET	4 PIECE	3.5H	1949-50	100
310	JAR	CHANG	10.5 H	1934-36	150
308	JAR	COOLIE	11H	1934-38	75
308D	JAR	COOLIE	11H	1942-46	100
365	JAR	DART CANDY	6.25D	1936-37	75
606	JAR	ELEPHANT	9.75H	1947	200
364	JAR	ELITE	4.5H	1936	50
301	JAR	MING	7.25H	1934-36	125
609D	JAR	PELICAN	6.5H	1947	175
465	JAR	SNACK	7D	1939	95
P4	JARDINIERE	LA FLEUR	3D	1941-50	15
P5	JARDINIERE	LA FLEUR	4D	1941-50	15
P6	JARDINIERE	LA FLEUR	5D	1941-50	20
P7	JARDINIERE	LA FLEUR	6D	1941-50	25
P8	JARDINIERE	LA FLEUR	7D	1941-50	25
254	LAMPBASE	DRAPED SHAFT	21.5H	1935	100
258	LAMPBASE	FLUTED SHAFT	23.5H	1935	100
256	LAMPBASE	SQUARE SHAFT	22.5H	1935	100
252	LAMPBASE	SWIRL SHAFT	20.5H	1935	100
100	N/D				
121-24	N/D				
128-29	N/D				
134-39	N/D				
159-69	N/D				
182-199	N/D				
723	N/D				
728	N/D				
731	N/D				
735	N/D				
430	PITCHER	FERN LEAF	8H	1937-38	125
200	PITCHER	LG, ICE LIPPED	2 QT	1940-41	125
201	PITCHER	MD	1 QT	1940-41	95
202	PITCHER	SM	1 PINT	1940-41	75
673	PLANTER	BURRO	4.5H	1949-50	45
726	PLANTER	CART	5X5SQ	1950	UTD
701	PLANTER	CHINESE SQUARE	4.75H	1950	50
668D	PLANTER	DAFFODIL	5.25H	1949	75
669	PLANTER	DONKEY	7.5H	1949-50	75
710	PLANTER	DRAPE	7L	1950	45
655D	PLANTER	DUTCH SHOE	5L	1948	45
672	PLANTER	FAWN	5H	1949-50	45
704	PLANTER	GAZELLE	4.75H	1950	45
667	PLANTER	GOURD	5.5H	1949-50	20
670	PLANTER	POOCH	4H	1949-50	55
652D	PLANTER	PUPPY	6.75L	1948-49	50
671	PLANTER	RAM	4H	1949-50	45
656	PLANTER	SQUARE	3.5H	1948-50	15
732	PLANTER	SQUARE FLUTED	6SQ	1950	UTD
415	PLATE	APPLE BLOSSOM	11.5D	1937	50
715D	PLATE	BAMBOO CONSOLE	10.5D	1950	175
342	PLATE	COUPE SALAD	7.5D	1935	40
343	PLATE	COUPE SERVICE	12D	1935	55
387	PLATE	DAISY SALAD	7.5D	1936-37	20
339	PLATE	SQUARE SALAD	7.5SQ	1935	40
340	PLATE	SQUARE SERVICE	10.5 SQ	1935	50
344	PLATE	WILD ROSE	10X12	1935-36	125
149S	POT & SAUCER	LA FLEUR	3H	1938-50	15
150S	POT & SAUCER	LA FLEUR	4H	1938-50	15
151S	POT & SAUCER	LA FLEUR	5H	1938-50	15
152S	POT & SAUCER	LA FLEUR	6H	1938-50	15
690D	RANGE SET	DAISY	3PIECES	1949-50	75
RE4	REFRIGERATOR	BUTTER DISH		1940	75
RE5	REFRIGERATOR	CASSEROLE	8L	1940	75
RE2	REFRIGERATOR	OBLONG LEFT OVR		1940	65
RE6	REFRIGERATOR	ROUND LEFT OVER	6D	1940	60
RE7	REFRIGERATOR	ROUND LEFT OVER	5D	1940	55
RE8	REFRIGERATOR	ROUND LEFT OVER	4D	1940	50
RE3	REFRIGERATOR	SQUARE LEFT OVR		1940	65
RE1	REFRIGERATOR	WATER JUG	2 QT	1940	85
680	SALT & PEPPER	DAISY	4H	1949-50	25pr
3904	SCULPTURE	FRUIT GIRL	10H	1937-38	250
3801	SCULPTURE	HEAD, LG	11.5H	1936-38	275
3802	SCULPTURE	HEAD, SM	8.5H	1936-38	250
3903	SCULPTURE	KNEELING NUDE	7H	1935-37	300
3901	SCULPTURE	NESCIA	16H	1935-37	UTD
3902	SCULPTURE	SCARF DANCER	13H	1935-37	325
3906	SCULPTURE	SHEP. & FAWN	11.5H	1937-38	225
329	STAND	FOR VASE	3.5D	1934-37	40

No.	Type	Name	Size	Years	Price
702D	STRING HOLDER	CHINESE FACE	5.5H	1950	175
712D	STRINGHOLDER	MOUSE	8.5H	1950	175
681	SUGAR BOWL	DAISY	3H	1949-50	20
683	TEA POT	DAISY	6.25	1949-50	65
691D	TEA SET	DAISY	3PIECES	1949-50	125
401	TEAPOT TILE	COOLIE	5SQ	1937-38	85
400	TEAPOT TILE	GEISHA	5SQ	1937-38	85
539	URN	REGENCY	7H	1941	25
647	URN	TALL	13.5	1948-50	50
563	URN	URN	9H	1947-48	35
538	URN	WREATH	9H	1941-46, 1950	25
567	VASE		5H	1947	30
567D	VASE		5H	1942-46	40
515	VASE	ABBEY	7H	1940-50	25
516	VASE	ACADIA	7H	1940-50	25
486	VASE	ACANTHUS, LG	11H	1939-50	30
485	VASE	ACANTHUS, SM	8H	1939-40	45
101	VASE	ALPHA, LG	10H	1938-49	20
105	VASE	ALPHA, MD	8H	1938-40	20
109	VASE	ALPHA, SM	6H	1938-41	20
632	VASE	ANCHOR	7.5H	1948-49	40
517	VASE	ARDEN	7H	1940-50	30
455	VASE	ASTERS, LG	11.5H	1938-40	50
455D	VASE	ASTERS, LG	11.5H	1939	75
453	VASE	ASTERS, SM	8H	1938-39	40
453D	VASE	ASTERS, SM	8H	1939	60
315	VASE	ATHENIAN	9H	1934-36, 1947	55
520	VASE	BADEN	9H	1940-48	30
521	VASE	BALI	9H	1940-41	90
522	VASE	BARRE	9H	1940-50	30
718	VASE	BASKET WEAVE		1950	UTD
535	VASE	BERNE	9H	1941-46	45
102	VASE	BETA, LG	10H	1938-39	30
106	VASE	BETA, MD	8H	1938-40	30
110	VASE	BETA, SM	6H	1938-41	30
468	VASE	BIRD	7.5H	1939-40	40
468D	VASE	BIRD	7.5H	1947-49	65
497 D	VASE	BLACKAMOOR	7.5H	1940	150
497	VASE	BLACKAMOOR	7.5H	1940	80
584	VASE	BOOT	8H	1947	45
593	VASE	BOW KNOT	9H	1947-48	35
402	VASE	BOX	5.5H	1937-38	55
534	VASE	BOYNE	9H	1941-46	40
616D	VASE	CACTUS	6.5H	1947-50	65
639	VASE	CALLA	8.5H	1948	40
351	VASE	CAPRI	5.75H	1935-37	125
325	VASE	CHIEN	6.5H	1934-37, 47	55
698	VASE	CHINESE TERRACE	6H	1950	45
114	VASE	CLASSIC	10H	1939-46	40
115	VASE	CLASSIC	10H	1939-49	30
116	VASE	CLASSIC	10H	1939-49	30
119	VASE	CLASSIC	10H	1947-49	25
120	VASE	CLASSIC	10H	1947-49	30
150	VASE	CLASSIC	9H	1941-42	25
151	VASE	CLASSIC	9H	1941-42	25
117	VASE	CLASSIC, LG	10H	1940-49	45
118	VASE	CLASSIC, LG	10H	1940-46	35
152	VASE	CLASSIC, LG	9H	1941-46	20
153	VASE	CLASSIC, LG	9H	1941-46	40
154	VASE	CLASSIC, LG	9H	1941-46	20
155	VASE	CLASSIC, LG	9H	1941-46	25
156	VASE	CLASSIC, LG	9H	1942-46	15
130	VASE	CLASSIC, MD	8H	1940	40
131	VASE	CLASSIC, MD	8H	1940	30
132	VASE	CLASSIC, MD	8H	1940	40
133	VASE	CLASSIC, MD	8H	1940	30
170	VASE	CLASSIC, MD	7H	1941	25
171	VASE	CLASSIC, MD	7H	1941	40
172	VASE	CLASSIC, MD	7H	1941	25
173	VASE	CLASSIC, MD	7H	1941	40
174	VASE	CLASSIC, MD	7H	1941	60
175	VASE	CLASSIC, MD	7H	1941	15
140	VASE	CLASSIC, SM	5.5H	1940-41	40
141	VASE	CLASSIC, SM	5.5H	1940-41	30
142	VASE	CLASSIC, SM	5.5H	1940-41	40
143	VASE	CLASSIC, SM	5.5H	1940-41	30
405	VASE	CROSSPATCH	8H	1937-38	55
104	VASE	DELTA, LG	10H	1938	40
108	VASE	DELTA, MD	8H	1938-39	40
112	VASE	DELTA, SM	6H	1938-39	40
557	VASE	DRAPED	11H	1941-48	45
469	VASE	DUTCH BOY	8H	1939-40	75
470	VASE	DUTCH GIRL	8H	1939-40	75
352	VASE	ECHO	4H	1935-40	25
524	VASE FLOOR	EGRET, LG	17.5H	1940-50	185
524A	VASE FLOOR	EGRET, SAND JAR	18H	1940-50	220

No.	Type	Name	Size	Years	Price
487	VASE FLOOR	EGRET, SM	14H	1939-50	150
307	VASE	FAIRFIELD	11 H	1934-37	150
484	VASE	FAN	8.5	1939-50	15
420	VASE	FERN LEAF	7.25H	1937-38	65
421	VASE	FERN LEAF	8.75H	1937-38	85
422	VASE	FERN LEAF	10.25H	1937-39	95
433	VASE FLOOR	FERN LEAF	15H	1937-39	145
350	VASE	FLEUR	7H	1935-38, 1947	95
176	VASE	FLORAL	10H	1950	65
177	VASE	FLORAL	10H	1950	65
178	VASE	FLORAL	10H	1950	65
179	VASE	FLORAL	10H	1950	65
180	VASE	FLORAL	10H	1950	65
181	VASE	FLORAL	10H	1950	65
491	VASE	FLOWER HOLDING	5H	1940-50	25
550	VASE	FLUTED	11H	1941-50	30
103	VASE	GAMMA, LG	10H	1938-39	35
107	VASE	GAMMA, MD	8H	1938-39	35
111	VASE	GAMMA, SM	6H	1938-39	35
389	VASE	GERANIUM	7H	1936-37	55
553	VASE	GRECIAN	13H	1941-47	55
603	VASE FLOOR	GRECIAN	15H	1947-49	150
613	VASE FLOOR	GRECIAN PITCHER	15H	1947	150
659	VASE	HACKNEY	8.5H	1948-49	45
312	VASE	HAN	6 H	1934-49	25
438	VASE	HAN SQUARE	6SQ	1938-41	20
630	VASE	HANDLED	9H	1948-49	50
634	VASE	HEIRLOOM	6.5H	1948	45
496	VASE	HOLLYHOCK	7.5H	1940	30
496D	VASE	HOLLYHOCK	7H	1947-48	45
594	VASE	HOUR GLASS	9H	1947	30
511	VASE	IONIC	8L	1940-41	35
628D	VASE	IRIS	8H	1948-49	60
445	VASE	LACED CUFF, SM	8H	1938-39	50
446	VASE	LACED CUFF, LG	10H	1938-39	60
556	VASE	LARGE	12.5H	1941-46	55
458	VASE	LATTICE	5.5H	1939	45
459	VASE	LATTICE	10.25H	1939-41	55
600	VASE	LAUREL	12H	1947-49	90
443	VASE	LAUREL, LG	8H	1938-39	60
442	VASE	LAUREL, SM	5.5H	1938-39	50
302	VASE	LUNG	11H	1934-38	225
390	VASE	M GLORY, LG	10H	1936-39	50
391	VASE	M GLORY, MD	7.75H	1936-38	45
392	VASE	M GLORY, SM	5.5H	1936-38	40
373	VASE	MANHATTAN	12.5H	1936-37	115
464	VASE	MEDALLION	8H	1939-40	40
705	VASE	MODERN	8H	1950	45
319	VASE	MODERN #1	7.25 H	1934-36	90
327	VASE	MODERN #2	6H	1934-36	75
328	VASE	MODERN #3	4.5 H	1934-36	75
730	VASE	MODERN BUD	8.5H	1950	UTD
727	VASE	MRS. ANDREWS		1950	UTD
717	VASE	MRS. BIDWELL		1950	UTD
309	VASE	NEO CLASSIC	12.5H	1934-36	125
309D	VASE	NEO CLASSIC	12.5H	1934-36	150
706	VASE	OAK LEAF	9.25H	1950	55
706D	VASE	OAK LEAF	9.25H	1950	70
637	VASE	OBLONG	9H	1948-50	45
353	VASE	PENTHOUSE		1935-38	100
483	VASE	PETITE BUD	8H	1939-40	35
483D	VASE	PETITE BUD	7.75H	1947-49	45
577	VASE	PILLOW	7H	1947-50	20
591	VASE	PLEAT	10H	1947-48	35
635	VASE	POCKET	6H	1948	45
629D	VASE	POPPY	6.5H	1948-49	80
599	VASE	QUILTED	9H	1947-50	55
472	VASE	REEDED	8H	1939	65
372	VASE	RHYTHM	10H	1936-37	55
380	VASE	RHYTHM, MD	7.75H	1936-37	50
381	VASE	RHYTHM, SM	5.5H	1936-37	45
554	VASE	RIBBED	9H	1941-46	50
625	VASE	RIBBED	6.5H	1948	50
462	VASE	RIBBON BOWL	4.5H	1939-50	15
318	VASE	RING	10.25 H	1934-37	95
324	VASE	ROPE	6.25H	1934-38, 47-48	35
G3	VASE FLOOR	ROPE, LG	18H	1939-50	190
G4	VASE FLOOR	ROPE, SM	14H	1939-50	175
598D	VASE	ROSETTE	7.25H	1947-48	45
725	VASE	ROUND		1950	UTD
357	VASE	SALON	14H	1935-38	100
304	VASE	SANG	9.5 H	1934-36	65
566	VASE	SCALLOP	9H	1947-48	25
566D	VASE	SCALLOP	9H	1942-46	45
335	VASE	SCALLOPED	10.5L	1935-38	75
417	VASE	SCROLL	8H	1937-38	80

No.	Type	Name	Size	Years	Price
596D	VASE	SEAHORSE	8H	1947-48	60
507	VASE	SHELL OVAL	7.5H	1940-50	25
504	VASE	SHELL PLANTING	7.5H	1940-46	45
494	VASE	SHIP	7.5H	1940-46	30
494D	VASE	SHIP	7H	1947-49	45
703	VASE	SLANT TOP	9.5H	1950	85
492	VASE	SMALL BOWL	4H	1940	350
631	VASE	SQUARE	8H	1948-49	45
708	VASE	SQUARE LEAF	9H	1950	40
708D	VASE	SQUARE LEAF	9H	1950	80
552	VASE	SQUATTY	8.5D	1941-48	45
G2	VASE GARDEN	SQUATTY PALM	19.5X18	1939-50	240
463	VASE	STAR	7.5H	1939-50	25
314	VASE	SWEDISH	8.25 H	1934-36	85
514	VASE	SWIRL, LG	11H	1940-50	50
513	VASE	SWIRL, MD	9H	1940-50	35
512	VASE	SWIRL, SM	7H	1940-50	25
G1	VASE GARDEN	TALL OIL JAR	24HX14.5D	1938-50	275
626	VASE	TAPER	6H	1948-49	50
537	VASE	TASSEL	9H	1941	65
418	VASE	TRI RIBBED	5H	1937-38	50
636D	VASE	TRIANGULAR	6.25H	1948	55
597	VASE	TRUMPET	9H	1947	45
320	VASE	TULIP	4H	1936-1937	70
604D	VASE	TULIP	6H	1947-48	75
654	VASE	TULIP	6.5H	1948-49	75
563D	VASE	URN	9H	1942-46	50
412	VASE FLOOR	VOLUTE, LG	15H	1937-40	150
411	VASE	VOLUTE, MD	10.5H	1937-40	100
410	VASE	VOLUTE, SM	8H	1937-39	75
A1	VASE	WHAT NOT	3.5H	1940-41	65
A2	VASE	WHAT NOT	3.5H	1940-41	65
A3	VASE	WHAT NOT	3.5H	1940-41	65
A4	VASE	WHAT NOT	3.5H	1940-41	65
A5	VASE	WHAT NOT	3.5H	1940-41	65
A6	VASE	WHAT NOT	3.5H	1940-41	65
B1	VASE	WHAT NOT	5H	1940-41	75
B2	VASE	WHAT NOT	5H	1940-41	75
B3	VASE	WHAT NOT	5H	1940-41	75
B4	VASE	WHAT NOT	5H	1940-41	75
B5	VASE	WHAT NOT	5H	1940-41	75
B6	VASE	WHAT NOT	5H	1940-41	75
C1	VASE	WHAT NOT	4.5H	1940-41	95
C2	VASE	WHAT NOT	4.5H	1940-41	75
C3	VASE	WHAT NOT	4.5H	1940-41	75
C4	VASE	WHAT NOT	4.5H	1940-41	75
C5	VASE	WHAT NOT	4.5H	1940-41	75
C6	VASE	WHAT NOT	4.5H	1940-41	75
466	VASE	WHEEL HANDLE	8H	1939-41	45
467	VASE	WREATH	8H	1939-40	65
589	WALL BRACKET	ACANTHUS	7H	1947	65
648	WALL VASE	ACANTHUS	8.75H	1948-50	65
649	WALL BRACKET	ACANTHUS	8.75H	1948	65
699D	WALL VASE	APRON	6H	1950	115
676D	WALL VASE	BOOK	6.5H	1949	100
601D	WALL POCKET	BUTTERFLY	8.5H	1947-49	110
586D	WALL VASE	CALLA	9H	1947-48	40
711	WALL VASE	CARRIAGE LAMP	10H	1950	80
587	WALL BRACKET	CHERUB	7.5H	1947	75
379	WALL POCKET	DAISY	7.75D	1936-41	70
379D	WALL POCKET	DAISY	7.75D	1936-41	80
493	WALL POCKET	DOUBLE	8.5H	1940	110
489	WALL POCKET	DUTCH BOY	10H	1939	125
490	WALL POCKET	DUTCH GIRL	10H	1939	125
376F	WALL MASK	FEMALE, LG	7.5H	1936	200
378F	WALL MASK	FEMALE, SM	4.0H	1936	175
431	WALL POCKET	FERN LEAF	7.5H	1937-38	110
435	WALL POCKET	FERN LEAF TRI	8W	1938-40	125
457	WALL POCKET	IONIC	9H	1939	100
590D	WALL POCKET	IVY	7H	1947	65
724	WALL POCKET	LEAF	10X5.5L	1950	UTD
376M	WALL MASK	MALE, LG	7.5H	1936	200
378M	WALL MASK	MALE, SM	4.0H	1936	175
675D	WALL VASE	MATCH BOX	5.5H	1949-50	90
375	WALL POCKET	MORNING GLORY DOUBLE	6.5H	1936-40	45
377	WALL POCKET	MORNING GLORY	7.5H	1936-50	35
508	WALL POCKET	SHELL	7H	1940	90
640	WALL POCKET	TRIAD	8X5.5	1948-50	40
113	WATER JUG			1938	100
570	WINDOW BOX		10L	1947-50	15
570D	WINDOW BOX		10L	1942-46	20
721	WINDOW BOX		12.5L	1950	UTD
498	WINDOW BOX	HAN, LG	14.5L	1940-41	20
477	WINDOW BOX	LG	13.5L	1939-41	35
576	WINDOW BOX	LG	12.25L	1947-50	25
476	WINDOW BOX	MD	10.5L	1939-50	30
729	WINDOW BOX	SCROLL END		1950	UTD
475	WINDOW BOX	SM	7L	1939-40	25
448	WINDOW BOX	SUNBURST	9L	1938-39	40

INDEX

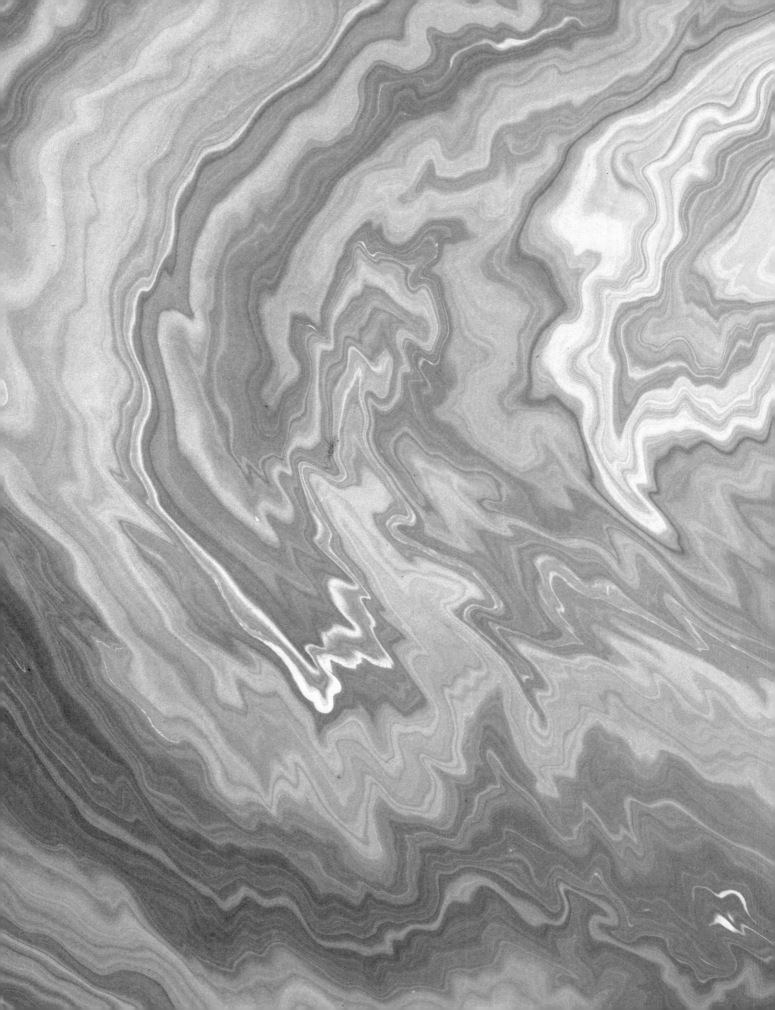